CW00540354

Day Wa....
HighWeald

20 circular routes in Sussex & Kent

Vertebrate Publishing, Sheffield
www.v-publishing.co.uk

Day Walks on the HighWeald

20 circular routes in Sussex & Kent

Deirdre Huston

Day Walks on the HighWeald

20 circular routes in
Sussex & Kent

VP First published in 2018 by Vertebrate Publishing.

Vertebrate Publishing, Crescent House, 228 Psalter Lane, Sheffield S11 8UT, United Kingdom.
www.v-publishing.co.uk

Copyright © 2018 Deirdre Huston and Vertebrate Publishing Ltd.

Deirdre Huston has asserted her rights under the Copyright, Designs and Patents Act 1988 to be identified as author of this work.

A CIP catalogue record for this book is available from the British Library.

ISBN 978-1-911342-85-4

Front cover: A coastal path in Hastings Country Park (route 19).
Back cover: View across fields to an oast house (route 14).
All photography by Deirdre Huston.

All maps reproduced by permission of Ordnance Survey on behalf of The Controller of Her Majesty's Stationery Office. © Crown Copyright. 100025218.

Design and production by Nathan Ryder.
Printed and bound in Europe by Pulsio.
Vertebrate Publishing is committed to printing on paper from sustainable sources.

MIX
Paper from
responsible sources
FSC® C128169
FSC
www.fsc.org

Contents

* Shortcut available

VANGUARD WAY NEAR HIGH HURSTWOOD (ROUTE 10)

Introduction

Join me on a journey to explore the High Weald.

Get fit. Stay fit. Enjoy the physical experience of putting one foot in front of the other. Venture out alone and immerse yourself in observing your surroundings or take company and enjoy exploring together.

Walk down old coach roads. Clamber through deserted woodland and along riverbanks. March past castles and ruined manors. Skirt battlefields. Linger in meadows. Leap across Wealden streams and climb gentle hills. See the landscape which inspired writers like Milne and Kipling or tramp up sunken lanes formed by early pig-drovers. The lie of the land leaves clues to our past. The iron and wool industries have left their marks. Unearth settlements, homes and churches. Let the facts emerge but take one step further: discover the High Weald's ever-evolving character and gain a greater sensibility of how people used to live. Let the landscape be our link between different times; an ironmaster's house once echoed with the hum of activity but now appears isolated. A trickling stream endures, the stone bricks of a bridge disappear beneath moss, rough cobbles slow our steps, ferns cling to rock and spring flowers creep up a steep-sided gill. How the seasons offer up change.

Stop at centuries-old pubs and characterful cafes, or picnic where the irregular fields stretch out to embrace a fickle sky. Food is an important part of a day walk and I have provided information on refreshments to help you plan. Local producers grow crops, make wine or raise livestock. Tourism plays its part. The High Weald story is not yet over. What must we do to preserve the rare heaths, enable meadows to buzz with invertebrates and help ancient woodlands to retain their character?

The lives of both individuals and communities are shaped by the fortunes of this region and there are plenty of tales waiting to be told. Some still wait to unfold. What will be the story of your *day walk*?

I hope you enjoy these trails as much as I have.

Deirdre Huston

Acknowledgements

Researching, exploring and route testing would not have been half as much fun without my son, Sean, with his infectious enthusiasm and eye for detail; husband, Ian, who quietly helps whenever help is needed and always enjoys a walk; daughter, Tegan, with her indomitable humour in the face of stinging nettles; Rory, with his video skills; and friends Bev and Carol for valuable advice and good company. Gösta Luthman's encouragement got the guidebook off to a flying start. Other diligent testers included Sue and Simon Mills, Steve Turner, LDWA walks leader Susanne Waldschmidt, and my father, Bob Huston, with whom I enjoyed discussing the High Weald Landscape Trail.

Thank you all xx

About the walks

The day walks in this book are divided geographically into four sections and then listed in ascending order of distance. This does not necessarily mean that the longest distance walks will take the longest time. All are designed as 'day' walks inasmuch as it is not intended that anyone will attempt more than one in a day.

Walk times

Stating the obvious, walkers' fitness levels, walking speeds and interests all vary and the time given is very approximate. Some walkers will want to visit every church, look in shops, take photographs and spend awhile at a lunch stop. Perhaps the best advice is to try one of the shorter walks, starting early enough so that you aren't caught out after dark; compare your time with the time suggested, then adjust times accordingly.

Navigation

This book refers to Ordnance Survey 1:25,000-scale maps of which OL34, 124, 125, 135, 136 have been used. It should not be necessary to refer to one of these while walking; the book map and directions should be sufficient. However, some walkers may wish or need to vary the routes, which is when the OS map will be required. In most cases the compass points are not used in route descriptions, but having a compass handy is not a bad idea.

The five OS maps in the 1:25,000 Explorer series we use are:

OL34 Crawley & Horsham
124 Hastings & Bexhill
125 Romney Marsh, Rye & Winchelsea
135 Ashdown Forest
136 High Weald

GPS and mobile phones

Both have their place but neither can be relied upon and it can be good to have a break from technology. GPS can be useful, but, quite seriously, despite the High Weald being a civilised area, there are many places where there is no phone reception and many wooded stretches where your GPS will lose signal. Remember to charge the batteries!

Footpaths and rights of way

Rights of way have been taken from the Ordnance Survey 1:25,000 maps. For the most part, paths, including permissive paths, are marked on the ground with appropriate signage. All these are, however, subject to change. Where signs ask you to walk around rather than through a crop or livestock, please respect the landowner's wishes.

Comfort

A decent pair of boots will protect your feet from the kind of terrain experienced in the High Weald and will also provide ankle support, waterproofing and grip on slippery or uneven tracks. Wealden clay is notoriously sticky! Surfaces alter with the seasons and some paths can be very muddy. Remember it only takes a short stretch of path to make your feet wet and we cannot predict mud levels as they fluctuate.

Occasionally paths may be overgrown and long trousers are advised. A waterproof jacket could be useful on any day at any time of year. A pack containing a waterproof, spare layer and some food and drink will make any day more comfortable. Remember, refreshment stops can be unexpectedly closed. Anybody with joint problems, for example ankles or knees, will probably benefit from a pair of trekking poles. These poles are also useful for stability where paths are uneven or slippery.

Safety

In general, the High Weald is kind. It's not rugged, wild country, but some paths can be surprisingly isolated and accidents can happen to anyone. Stay away from cliff edges as erosion is not always obvious and can be fatal. Wear suitable footwear. Carry enough drinking water and wear sun cream. Planning can help to prevent incidents. Winter walking is enjoyable, but immobility caused by a fall could soon result in hypothermia. Always ensure you have sufficient warm clothing, and, especially if walking alone, consider a whistle and emergency blanket or bivvy bag which will take very little space in your rucksack. If possible, tell someone where you are going.

Long sleeves and trousers, closed shoes and some insect repellent can all help protect you against insect bites. Particularly if walking through grazing fields or dense vegetation, be aware that ticks can be a problem. Ticks can carry diseases, including Lyme disease, and if you find a tick, seek advice from the NHS (**www.nhs.uk**) or the charity Lyme Disease Action (**www.lymediseaseaction.org.uk**).

Rescue

In the case of an emergency dial **999** and ask for **Police**. Where possible give a six-figure grid reference of your location or that of the casualty. If you don't have reception where you are, try and attract the help of others around you. The usual distress signal is six short blasts on a whistle every minute. If you don't have a whistle, then shouting may work.

Emergency rescue by SMS text

Another option in the UK is contacting the emergency services by SMS text – useful if you have a low battery or intermittent signal, but you do need to register your phone first. To register, simply text '**register**' to **999** and then follow the instructions in the reply. **Do it now** – it could save yours or someone else's life. **www.emergencysms.org.uk**

The Countryside Code

Respect other people

Please respect the local community and other people using the outdoors. Remember your actions can affect people's lives and livelihoods.

Consider the local community and other people enjoying the outdoors

» Respect the needs of local people and visitors alike – for example, don't block gateways, driveways or other paths with your vehicle.
» When riding a bike or driving a vehicle, slow down or stop for horses, walkers and farm animals and give them plenty of room. By law, cyclists must give way to walkers and horse riders on bridleways.
» Co-operate with people at work in the countryside. For example, keep out of the way when farm animals are being gathered or moved and follow directions from the farmer.
» Busy traffic on small country roads can be unpleasant and dangerous to local people, visitors and wildlife – so slow down and, where possible, leave your vehicle at home, consider sharing lifts and use alternatives such as public transport or cycling. For public transport information, phone Traveline on 0871 200 22 33 or visit **www.traveline.info**

Leave gates and property as you find them and follow paths unless wider access is available

» A farmer will normally close gates to keep farm animals in, but may sometimes leave them open so the animals can reach food and water. Leave gates as you find them or follow instructions on signs. When in a group, make sure the last person knows how to leave the gates.
» Follow paths unless wider access is available, such as on open country or registered common land (known as 'open access' land).
» If you think a sign is illegal or misleading such as a *Private – No Entry* sign on a public path, contact the local authority.
» Leave machinery and farm animals alone – don't interfere with animals even if you think they're in distress. Try to alert the farmer instead.
» Use gates, stiles or gaps in field boundaries if you can – climbing over walls, hedges and fences can damage them and increase the risk of farm animals escaping.
» Our heritage matters to all of us – be careful not to disturb ruins and historic sites.

Protect the natural environment

We all have a responsibility to protect the countryside now and for future generations, so make sure you don't harm animals, birds, plants or trees and try to leave no trace of your visit. When out with your dog make sure it is not a danger or nuisance to farm animals, horses, wildlife or other people.

Leave no trace of your visit and take your litter home

» Protecting the natural environment means taking special care not to damage, destroy or remove features such as rocks, plants and trees. They provide homes and food for wildlife, and add to everybody's enjoyment of the countryside.

» Litter and leftover food doesn't just spoil the beauty of the countryside, it can be dangerous to wildlife and farm animals – so take your litter home with you. Dropping litter and dumping rubbish are criminal offences.

» Fires can be as devastating to wildlife and habitats as they are to people and property – so be careful with naked flames and cigarettes at any time of the year. Sometimes, controlled fires are used to manage vegetation, particularly on heaths and moors between 1 October and 15 April, but if a fire appears to be unattended then report it by calling **999**.

Keep dogs under effective control

When you take your dog into the outdoors, always ensure it does not disturb wildlife, farm animals, horses or other people by keeping it under effective control. This means that you:

» keep your dog on a lead, or

» keep it in sight at all times, be aware of what it's doing and be confident it will return to you promptly on command

» ensure it does not stray off the path or area where you have a right of access

Special dog rules may apply in particular situations, so always look out for local signs – for example:

» dogs may be banned from certain areas that people use, or there may be restrictions, byelaws or control orders limiting where they can go

» the access rights that normally apply to open country and registered common land (known as 'open access' land) require dogs to be kept on a short lead between 1 March and 31 July, to help protect ground-nesting birds, and all year round near farm animals

» at the coast, there may also be some local restrictions to require dogs to be kept on a short lead during the bird breeding season, and to prevent disturbance to flocks of resting and feeding birds during other times of year

It's always good practice (and a legal requirement on 'open access' land) to keep your dog on a lead around farm animals and horses, for your own safety and for the welfare of the animals. A farmer may shoot a dog which is attacking or chasing farm animals without being liable to compensate the dog's owner.

However, if cattle or horses chase you and your dog, it is safer to let your dog off the lead – don't risk getting hurt by trying to protect it. Your dog will be much safer if you let it run away from a farm animal in these circumstances and so will you.

Everyone knows how unpleasant dog mess is and it can cause infections, so always clean up after your dog and get rid of the mess responsibly – 'bag it and bin it'. Make sure your dog is wormed regularly to protect it, other animals and people.

Enjoy the outdoors

Even when going out locally, it's best to get the latest information about where and when you can go. For example, your rights to go on to some areas of open access land and coastal land may be restricted in particular places at particular times. Find out as much as you can about where you are going, plan ahead and follow advice and local signs.

Plan ahead and be prepared

You'll get more from your visit if you refer to up-to-date maps or guidebooks and websites before you go. Visit **www.gov.uk/natural-england** or contact local information centres or libraries for a list of outdoor recreation groups offering advice on specialist activities.

You're responsible for your own safety and for others in your care – especially children – so be prepared for natural hazards, changes in weather and other events. Wild animals, farm animals and horses can behave unpredictably if you get too close, especially if they're with their young – so give them plenty of space.

Check weather forecasts before you leave. Conditions can change rapidly especially on mountains and along the coast, so don't be afraid to turn back. When visiting the coast check for tide times on **www.ukho.gov.uk/easytide** – don't risk getting cut off by rising tides and take care on slippery rocks and seaweed.

Part of the appeal of the countryside is that you can get away from it all. You may not see anyone for hours, and there are many places without clear mobile phone signals, so let someone else know where you're going and when you expect to return.

Follow advice and local signs
England has about 190,000 kilometres (118,000 miles) of public rights of way, providing many opportunities to enjoy the natural environment. Get to know the signs and symbols used in the countryside to show paths and open countryside.

Walking near livestock
Entering a field full of cattle can be intimidating, especially for those new to hillwalking. The Ramblers have advice on walking near livestock on their website: **www.ramblers.org. uk/advice/safety/walking-near-livestock.aspx**

How to use this book
This book should provide you with all of the information that you need for an enjoyable, trouble-free and successful walk. The following tips should also be of help:

1. We strongly recommend that you invest in the maps listed above on page ix. These are essential even if you are familiar with the area – you may need to cut short the walk or take an alternative route.
2. Choose your route. Consider the time you have available and the abilities/level of experience of all of members your party – then read the Safety section of this guide.
3. We recommend that you study the route description carefully before setting off. Cross-reference this with your map so that you've got a good sense of general orientation in case you need an alternative route. Make sure that you are familiar with the symbols used on the maps.
4. Get outdoors and enjoy walking!

Maps, descriptions, distances

While every effort has been made to maintain accuracy within the maps and descriptions in this guide, we have had to process a vast amount of information and we are unable to guarantee that every single detail is correct. Please exercise caution if a direction appears at odds with the route on the map. If in doubt, a comparison between the route, the description and a quick cross-reference with your map (along with a bit of common sense) should help ensure that you're on the right track.

Note that distances have been measured off the map, and map distances rarely coincide 100% with distances on the ground. Please treat stated distances as a guideline only. Ordnance Survey maps are the most commonly used, are easy to read and many people are happy using them. If you're not familiar with OS maps and are unsure of what the symbols mean, you can download a free OS 1:25,000 map legend from **www.ordnancesurvey.co.uk**

Here are a few of the symbols and abbreviations we use on the maps and in our directions:

 ROUTE STARTING POINT ROUTE MARKER  OPTIONAL ROUTE

 SHORTCUT   DIRECTIONAL ARROW

52 ADDITIONAL GRID LINE NUMBERS TO AID NAVIGATION

(P)BW = (Public) Bridleway   **(P)FP** = (Public) Footpath   **GR** = Grid reference
LHS/LH = Left-hand side/Left-hand   **RHS/RH** = Right-hand side/Right-hand **(!)** = Caution

Km/mile conversion chart

METRIC TO IMPERIAL

1 kilometre [km]	1000 m	0.6214 mile
1 metre [m]	100 cm	1.0936 yd
1 centimetre [cm]	10 mm	0.3937 in
1 millimetre [mm]		0.03937 in

IMPERIAL TO METRIC

1 mile	1760 yd	1.6093 km
1 yard [yd]	3 ft	0.9144 m
1 foot [ft]	12 in	0.3048 m
1 inch [in]		2.54 cm

Long-distance trails

Sections of the following linear long-distance trails are used in our routes and are recommended for further exploration. In some instances, their names are abbreviated within the directions.

High Weald Landscape Trail (HWLT)
A 90-mile route that meanders through the AONB from east to west, linking the ridge-top villages and historic gardens for which the area is famous.

Wealdway/Weald Way (WW)
An 80-mile-long path through Kent and Sussex conceived in 1970 by members of the Ramblers' Association (The Ramblers).

1066 Country Walk (1066 CW)
This 31-mile trail follows in the steps of William the Conqueror

Saxon Shore Way (SSW)
163 miles exploring the ancient coastline of Kent and East Sussex.

Sussex Border Path (SBP)
137 miles from Emsworth in Hampshire to Rye in East Sussex.

Further reading

The following is a selection of the books and websites which I drew upon while researching this guidebook. For more general information about the High Weald Area of Outstanding Natural Beauty, please visit: **www.highweald.org**

Weir Wood Reservoir and Brambletye House (route 2)
Ewing, Garen, *Brambletye House* [online] <http://www.garenewing.co.uk/home/collections/brambletye.html>

Horsfield, Thomas Walker, *The History, Antiquities, and Topography of the County of Sussex* (Lewes: Sussex Press, 1835).

St Leonard's Forest (route 3)

'1614, August: The Dragon of St. Leonard's Forest' on *Anomolies* [online] <http://anomalyinfo.com/Stories/1614-august-dragon-st-leonards-forest>

Ardingly (routes 4 and 5)

'Parishes: Balcombe' from *A History of the County of Sussex: Volume 7, the Rape of Lewes.* Salzman, L.F, ed, (London: Victoria County History, 1940), 132–136. *British History Online.* [online] <http://www.british-history.ac.uk/vch/sussex/vol7/pp132-136>

Eridge Rocks and Broadwater Warren (route 7)

'Eridge Rocks' on *Sussex Wildlife Trust* [online] <https://sussexwildlifetrust.org.uk/visit/eridge-rocks>

'Broadwater Warren' on *RSPB* [online] <https://www.rspb.org.uk/reserves-and-events/reserves-a-z/broadwater-warren>

Mayfield (route 8)

Bell-Irving, E.M., *Mayfield: The Story of an Old Wealden Village* (London: William Clowes and Sons, 1903).

Mayfield Village Walk Leaflet, featuring information from *Short Guide to Mayfield Past and Present* (Mayfield Local History Society).

Ashdown Forest (route 10)

Hodgkinson, Jeremy, *The Wealden Iron Industry* (Stroud: The History Press, 2008).

'Brickfield Meadow' on *Sussex Wildlife Trust* [online] <https://sussexwildlifetrust.org.uk/visit/brickfield-meadow>

Burwash (route 11)

'Puck of Pook's Hill' on *The Kipling Society* [online] <http://www.kiplingsociety.co.uk/rg_puck_intro.htm>

Kipling, Rudyard, 'Puck of Pook's Hill' originally published in *The Strand Magazine* (London: 1906).

Goudhurst (route 13)

Platt, Richard, *Smuggling in the British Isles: A History* (Stroud: Tempus Publishing, 2007).

Robertsbridge (route 17)

About Robertsbridge [online] <http://www.aboutrobertsbridge.org.uk>

'The Abbey' on Historic England [online] <https://www.historicengland.org.uk/listing/the-list/list-entry/1221354>

Battle (route 18)

'Hastings 1066: The Battle' on *The History Press* [online] <www.thehistorypress.co.uk/articles/hastings-1066-the-battle>

'History of our Church' on *Saint George's Crowhurst* [online] <www.stgeorgescrowhurst.org.uk/history>

Hastings (route 19)

Reminiscences of Smugglers and Smuggling by John Banks of Hastings, p.3, published by John Camden Hotten, 1873, Quote by permission of the British Library, Shelfmark 8246.aa.6

'Hastings Country Park' on *High Weald* [online] <http://www.highweald.org/explore-sussex/nature-reserves/2154-hastings-country-park.html>

'Hastings Country Park Local Nature Reserve' on *Hastings Online* [online] <https://www.hastings.gov.uk/countryside_nature/naturereserves/naturereserves_hastings/hcp>

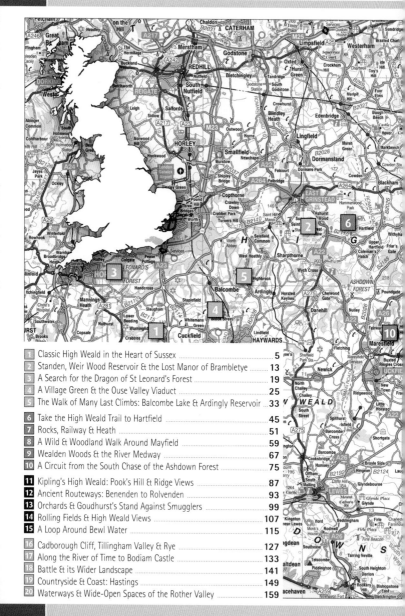

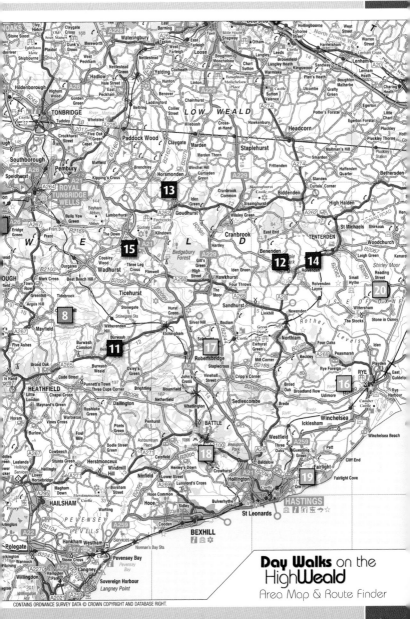

Day Walks on the
HighWeald
Area Map & Route Finder

CONTAINS ORDNANCE SURVEY DATA © CROWN COPYRIGHT AND DATABASE RIGHT.

SECTION 1

West High Weald

Once you start looking for the characteristic rolling hills, shaws and streams of the High Weald, it may alter how you perceive this area of Sussex and Surrey. The western end of the Weald Forest Ridge holds its ground in the remaining green space between several towns which makes the peace and relaxation it offers all the more valuable. The ancient forest of St Leonard's retains a feel of woodland tranquillity. Much of the land is used to raise livestock; paths and tracks tend to be well defined. You may find yourself walking through a vineyard as High Weald soil and climate suit the vine. Recent history in the form of glittering reservoirs and Victorian engineering seems to dominate this landscape but, look carefully, and there are plenty of clues to a more distant past of lost manors and Iron Age prosperity, fulling mills and martyrs.

VIEW OVER FIELDS AND WOODLAND NEAR STANDEN (ROUTE 2)

THE LAKE NEAR SLAUGHAM

01 Classic High Weald in the Heart of Sussex

13.5km/8.4miles

A simple circuit through classic High Weald scenery with well-established paths, lakeside views and a chance to enjoy a little history.

Bolney » Wykehurst Park » High Weald Landscape Trail » Slaugham Manor lake » Slaugham » Warninglid » Bolney

Start

Batchelor's Field car park at Rawson Hall, off The Street, Bolney. GR: TQ 261231.

The Walk

This is a lovely, easy walk and it's hard not to be impressed by the peace and tranquillity of these Mid Sussex routeways. The landscape feels typically High Weald, especially where irregular low-rolling fields and copses or 'shaws' are interspersed with farmsteads. The lake near Slaugham is wild and natural and, if you have a camera, you may find inspiration here. Geese gather among the lily pads and their persistent honking may be the only sound disturbing the peace.

Choose to stop at The Half Moon in Warninglid or, if you prefer a picnic, look for a bench in the Woodland Trust's Church Covert, a native broadleaf woodland with a 1,000-year-old yew tree, a marshy meadow and a mill pond. Towards the end of the walk, Bolney Wine Estate is ideally situated for an exploratory visit to shop, cafe or vineyard. Over the last 35 years the sandstone soil has proved perfect for growing vines and this award-winning wine producer is raising the profile of English wine across the world.

Our diversion to Slaugham also enables you to glimpse the atmospheric ruins of Slaugham Place, a Tudor mansion, originally owned by one of the owners of Slaugham Furnace, Richard Covert. On inheriting, Sir Walter Covert rebuilt the house. In the south chapel of 13th-century St Mary's church, see a fine brass of 1503 remembering John Covert and a beautifully carved wall monument to Richard Covert and his individually named wives, sons and daughters.

Place names near Warninglid, such as Engine Pond, Furnace Pond and Minepits Wood, suggest links to the iron industry, while The Old Mill House is a restored timber-framed building which dates from the late 16th century. There appears to be little evidence of dramatic events in this area and perhaps inhabitants have always quietly prospered, but I doubt it. Life is rarely so simple.

CLASSIC HIGH WEALD IN THE HEART OF SUSSEX

DISTANCE: 13.5KM/8.4MILES » TOTAL ASCENT: 286M/938FT » START GR: TQ 261231 » TIME: ALLOW 3.5 HOURS PLUS STOPS » SATNAV: RH17 5PG » MAP: OS EXPLORER OL34, CRAWLEY & HORSHAM, 1:25,000 » REFRESHMENTS: THE HALF MOON, WARNINGLID; CAFE AND SHOP, BOLNEY WINE ESTATE » NAVIGATION: STRAIGHTFORWARD, WELL-SIGNED PATHS.

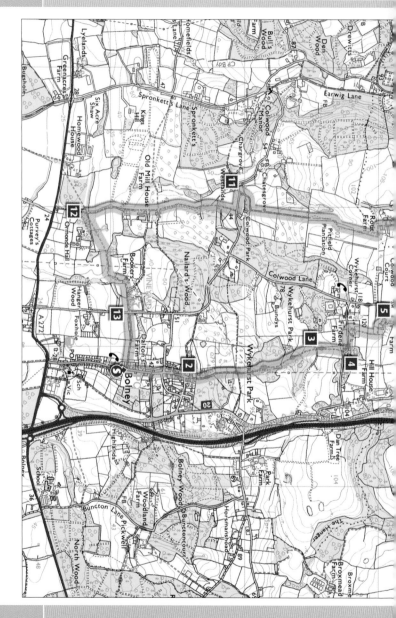

**01 CLASSIC HIGH
WEALD IN THE HEART
OF SUSSEX**

Directions – Classic High Weald in the Heart of Sussex

➎ As you leave the car park, **turn right** at the entrance along the signed tarmac path past the play area. **Exit left** through the barriers and **turn right** along The Street. Walk up the hill. Pass Cherry Lane, Lodge Lane, Tythe Barn and a signpost.

2 Walk **straight ahead**, following the signed public footpath as you leave Top Street to continue up the hill. Pass **straight ahead** through the gap beside a waymarked gate to follow the footpath. This is the High Weald Landscape Trail (HWLT), although unsigned. Walk **straight on** past a signpost where the track narrows. Follow the footpath along a fence. Go through a bridge. Walk **straight on** at two signposts close together. The wooded path passes between grazing fields. **Bear left** past a pylon, **beware** uneven ground as you descend. Cross a plank bridge and continue on. **Easy to miss**: keep **straight on** where the path forks: **do not** walk past the marker post inscribed *PRIVATE*. This pleasant path descends through woodland. Cross a footbridge and go **diagonally left** to a waymarked signpost. Pass a barrier and walk **diagonally right** past a waymarked signpost. At the edge of the open field, pass another signpost and continue onwards.

3 Cross the private road at the signpost, walking **slightly right** to cross a stile and follow the signed footpath **diagonally right**. Climb the steepish hill keeping to the **right** of the house. Cross a stile.

4 Walk **left** along the lane. **Turn right** at the signpost after The Old Distillery. After a few steps, **walk left** following the signed footpath up the narrow track along the fence. Go through a kissing gate and follow the footpath **slightly diagonally left** to climb over the stile. **Easy to miss**: head **slightly diagonally left** again to cross a stile in the middle of the hedge. **Keep walking diagonally left**.

5 Cross the tarmac drive to the farm and follow the signed footpath **right** and then **straight along** the fence avoiding the pond. Go through a metal kissing gate and **follow the signed footpath onwards**, roughly along the line of the overhead wires. Go through a gate and **continue** along the signed footpath. Go through a second gate, across a footbridge and walk on along the fence. Cross a small footbridge and walk **straight on** past the signpost. **The path veers diagonally left** through the open field passing two more distant signposts. Pass another signpost in the corner of the field and **walk right** into North Gravelies Wood. **Turn left** at the next signpost, keeping to the public footpath. Pass yet another signpost and cross a stile. Walk **straight on making a diagonal path** across the field to the gate. At this crossroads of paths, **veer left** to walk **straight on** along the part-concrete drive and public footpath, past South Gate stables. Go over a cattle grid and walk on until the road.

6 Turn left for a short distance **taking care** when you cross busy Cuckfield Lane. **Turn right** at the signpost. Follow the footpath, enjoying views over woodland. In the corner, pass a signpost and walk into the woods. Pass a signpost and **veer left** past some huge trees and on through the woods. The HWLT is intermittently signed. Cross a footbridge and broken stile to follow the signed footpath **straight on** down through the meadow. Pass a signpost. **Walk on**, keeping the first two ponds and house on your left. Pass between the second and third ponds towards the signpost. Walk **straight on**, following the waymarked footpath across the meadow. **Turn left** at the signpost and walk on, keeping the hedge on your right. The path narrows and continues between fences. Pass a gate and follow the tarmac path onwards past Slaugham Place Farm and down the hill.

7 At the three-way signpost beside a large lake, walk **straight ahead** to visit the church, ruins of Slaugham Place or the pub. Pass the lake and **turn left** at the signpost to follow the fenced footpath to Slaugham along the water's edge. Pass a marker post and **walk right** along the path, away from the lake. At the end of the fence, **turn left** through Church Covert Woods to keep walking in the same direction until you reach the signpost in the churchyard. It is well worth exploring inside the church to see the brass engraving and poignant monument to individuals of the Covert family. To see the atmospheric ruins of their home, Slaugham Place, **turn right** at the signpost in the churchyard, then go through a gate and enter Church Covert. To gain a better glimpse of the ruins, walk **diagonally right** along the signed footpath and then continue through a gate and along a fenced footpath for a few steps. It's easy to imagine the scale and grandeur of the mansion in Tudor times.

Retrace your footsteps through Church Covert woods and past Slaugham lake. **Veer right** at the Slaugham Place Farm notice and signpost at Point 7 and walk on beside this unspoiled lake. **Turn left** over the waymarked stile.

8 **Turn right** at the signpost to cross a stile and a footbridge. Head up the field towards a concrete barn. Pass the signpost and part-stile. Walk **straight on** past the metal skeleton of an outbuilding and follow a narrow track along a fence and behind some brick buildings and onwards. Cross or pass a stile without a fence and pass a marker post. **Walk right**, heading away from the drive, on the grassy waymarked footpath towards the next marker post and onwards. Head up the open field, over the ridge and towards a kissing gate in the hedge.

9 **Turn left** along a pavement beside the road. Walk up the slope. Pass the crossroads and The Half Moon pub (unless you want to nip inside!). Walk on along The Street, passing a couple of footpaths. Go down the hill.

10 At Riflemans Cottage, walk **straight on** along the tarmac driveway and signed public bridleway. **Keep left** on the bridleway where the path forks: try to spot a signpost in the hedge on your left! Walk up the steep hill towards Rout Farm. Walk through the gate and **straight on** through the private sheep farm **staying on the public bridleway**. After the first green barn, **go left** by the big tree trunk to follow the clearly signed and fenced public bridleway past the sheep enclosure. **Turn right** and stay on the signed, fenced bridleway. Pass a pond on your right. Pass a stile and a High Weald Circular Walks marker post. Continue on along the narrow footpath with fine views towards the South Downs. Go through a gate and walk on along the fenced path and down the hill. Near the house, **walk straight on**, keeping the conifer hedge and barn on your right. Walk between a hedge and a fence, passing a signpost. **Turn right** along the tarmac drive. Follow the bridleway past another signpost and along past several houses.

11 **Turn left** along the lane for about 100m. **Turn right** at the signpost, walk through the kissing gate and descend through pleasing open woodland for a short distance. Pass through another kissing gate into denser woodland. The track feels reminiscent of an old sunken path, with cobbles and its proximity to the stream, an ancient routeway perhaps to the old mill. Emerge at a path junction by Old Mill House. Follow the signed public footpath **straight on** along the tarmac lane.

12 At the signpost, **turn left** along the public footpath. At the next signpost, go through the gate and walk along the footpath beside the posts towards the gate. Go through the kissing gate **on the left** following the signed footpath **diagonally left**. At the signpost, go through two gates and pass a waymarked post, walking **straight ahead** along the footpath through the vineyard. In the corner, go through another high deer gate and walk up the hill along the waymarked footpath towards a distant rooftop. Cross the stile. **Note**: no access to vineyard here but soon. Walk on a few steps then **head right** along the gravel track. Walk **straight ahead** at the signpost, staying on the public footpath, and pass between a couple more vineyards.

13 **At the road, you have a choice**. If you wish to visit the vineyard cafe or shop, **turn left** up the lane and then **left again** as signed. Otherwise, cross the road and walk **straight on** along the signed footpath. **Turn left** at the next road to return to the car park.

A SCULPTURE OF THE COVERT FAMILY

STANDEN, WEIR WOOD RESERVOIR & THE LOST MANOR OF BRAMBLETYE

DISTANCE: 14KM/8.7MILES » **TOTAL ASCENT**: 203M/667FT » **START GR**: TQ 426350 » **TIME**: ALLOW 3–3.5 HOURS PLUS STOPS » **SATNAV**: RH18 5HE » **MAP**: OS EXPLORER 135, ASHDOWN FOREST, 1:25,000 » **REFRESHMENTS**: TABLEHURST FARM CAFE AND THE OLD DUNNINGS MILL, EAST GRINSTEAD; STANDEN HOUSE NT CAFE; OPTIONS IN FOREST ROW INCLUDE TAFFELS CAFE (RECOMMENDED!) » **NAVIGATION**: ONE UNSIGNED BUT STRAIGHTFORWARD SECTION AFTER HORSESHOE FARM.

BRAMBLETYE MANOR RUINS GLIMPSED FROM FOREST WAY

Standen, Weir Wood Reservoir & the Lost Manor of Brambletye

14km/8.7miles

A satisfying circuit over varied terrain with lots to see and do, peaceful moments and a little history: a good introduction to High Weald walking.

Forest Row » Forest Way » East Grinstead » High Weald Landscape Trail » Standen » Weir Wood Reservoir » Brambletye House ruins » Forest Way » Forest Row

Start

Lower Road car park, off Station Road. Free parking in long- and medium-stay bays. GR: TQ 426350. Alternative: Hartfield Road Car Park with public toilets if community centre open.

The Walk

The walk begins with a two-and-a-half-kilometre stretch along Forest Way. This disused railway trail enables you to gain some height with little effort while enjoying a purposeful atmosphere. The path provides a popular corridor for both people and wildlife, and this may be an ideal walk for those who don't like to stray too far from civilisation.

The next stretch is through farmland where a wonderful feeling of space makes for a tranquil mood. At the road, we join a pleasing stretch of the High Weald Landscape Trail which escapes past a few houses to meander through fields and copse before looping around Standen House. Do try and pop into this National Trust property. Not only is the house renowned for its associations with William Morris and the Arts and Craft Movement, but on one visit here I was struck by the sense of a welcoming 1920s family home and the enthusiasm

with which modern inventions, such as electricity, were embraced.

Wander on down to the reservoir to walk along its northerly side. Be warned: this path can become muddy! Once, this High Weald valley was an important iron-producing area and it seems apt that the last part of the route follows a stream back towards Forest Way.

This last section of the walk has a real feel of the High Weald. Look out for the ruins of Brambletye Manor. First mentioned in the Domesday Book, the original manor house appears to have been replaced by a Jacobean structure which features in the 1826 novel *Brambletye House; or, Cavaliers and Roundheads: A Novel*, now available on the Internet Archive. The Domesday Book records: *'Ralph holds Brambertei of the Earl. Cola held it of King Edward. It has constantly been rated at one hide. The arable is one plough land and a half. Here is a priest with a villain, one plough and a half and thirteen bondsmen. A wood and herbage yield twelve hogs. There are five acres of meadow, and a mill of two shillings. In the reign of the Confessor the value was thirty shillings; the present estimate is twenty.'*

Directions – Standen, Weir Wood Reservoir & the Lost Manor of Brambletye

⮕ Leave the car park through the metal bike barriers and cross Station Road to join the bridleway at the wooden waymarker. Follow the path through a children's play area. At the second bench, **turn left** passing the skateboard ramps to walk along a tree-lined mud track. At the three-way wooden waymarker **turn left** along the bridleway. Keep **straight ahead** at the next wooden signpost staying on the bridleway to cross the bridge. Upon joining Forest Way, **turn left** towards East Grinstead. Take the **right-hand track** as signed on the small blue National Cycle Network 21 arrow on the post which soon ascends to a tarmac lane.

2 **Turn left** along Forest Way. Walk along this tarmac lane. Pass a veterinary centre and a water treatment works. Cross a main road on a pedestrian crossing and continue along this path towards East Grinstead for just over 2km, crossing the minor road at Brambletye along the way.

3 **Easy to miss: turn left**, not more than 75m before a railway bridge on a small path which veers off up the bank away from Forest Way to follow the waymarked Sussex Border Path (SBP). **Turn left** to follow the signed footpath along the quiet lane. Weir Wood Reservoir can be seen ahead. Pass Horseshoe Cottage.

4 At the signpost, **turn right**. Cross the footbridge, go through the metal gate and walk **straight ahead**. Wander up through the unsigned middle of this vast grassy field heading for a walkers' metal gate in the far right top corner. Continue to the far right-hand corner of the next field. Pass through a gate and head across the paddock.

5 **Turn right** at the gate and signposts along the byway towards East Grinstead. At Boyles Farmhouse, keep **straight ahead** on the now gravelled byway. Beyond Dairy Cottage, **turn left** through the walkers' gate to follow the waymarked footpath. Head diagonally across the field and pass through the wooden gate. **Immediately turn left** and soon cross a narrow footbridge. Continue along a path between the fence and stream. Go through a metal barrier and along a tarmac path past a playground.

02 STANDEN, WEIR WOOD RESERVOIR & THE LOST MANOR OF BRAMBLETYE

Directions – Standen, Weir Wood Reservoir & the Lost Manor of Brambletye continued...

6 Emerge on Dunnings Road opposite The Old Dunnings Mill. **Walk left** along the pavement, **ignoring** a footpath signed up Streatfield Place, and then **turn right** along the signed footpath. The *No public right of way* sign applies to traffic only. At Medway Drive, **turn left** following the footpath signing the High Weald Landscape Trail (HWLT) and Standen Trail. After a few houses, go past a gatepost and **straight ahead** across some fields. Climb gradually, passing a signpost, walking along the edge of the field. Head into the trees and follow the unsigned mud and grass track through the copse. Eventually it runs along a fence. Soon the path climbs between two banks of trees towards a waymarker. At the rugby ground **turn left** along the footpath which exits the field just beyond the pylon.

7 At the road, **turn left** for a short distance. **Turn right** towards Standen following the HWLT and Standen Trail. Divert into Standen House or cafe if you wish. Otherwise, at the waymarkers, **turn right** to follow the HWLT, keeping on the mud track beside the fence. A vista showcases the Weald to your right and there's a handy picnic bench. Go through a kissing gate and follow the **left-hand path** down through the field and towards the reservoir. At a signpost, walk **straight ahead** descending on a track between tree banks and continue past the next signpost. At the third signpost, **keep right** and go through the metal gate. Follow the signed footpath towards the reservoir.

8 Beside the reservoir, **turn left** to join the signed footpath and, as an overview, keep on this path around the reservoir until you pass beyond the far end. Keep **straight ahead** at the next signpost. The path leads away from the water (turning left). Cross a stile and continue along a mud track and across a plank bridge. Walk **straight on** along the fenced track. Pass a bench from which there are views of the reservoir. At the signpost keep **straight ahead**. Cross a stile and follow the curved line of the field. At the signpost, go **straight ahead** through one wooden gate and then two more. Cross a footbridge. The track wends through a woodland and follows the line of a fence. Keep **straight ahead** at the next two signposts. Your path follows the mesh fence around the reservoir, passing an occasional bench or noticeboard. See the waterworks and sluice in the distance. Go through a gate into a field and go **straight ahead** along the fence. Ignore the Millenium Walk and continue **straight ahead** on the public footpath. At the edge of the field pass the sign and go through a metal kissing gate. Cross a stile and continue along the fenced track. This path may be muddy. Pass metal gates and continue on to cross a footbridge over a stream.

9 At the three-way signpost, **turn left** and walk along the stream. Cross over another footbridge and walk on. **Turn right** on a footpath, walking on through the aptly named Orchard Eggs Farmhouse. Continue on the byway passing Brambletye Manor Barn B&B. Stay on the track as it curves left following the footpath sign and passing Brambletye Manor Farmhouse. Keep an eye out for the ruins (no access). Walk on along this quiet lane until you reach Brambletye Crossing.

10 **Turn right** back along Forest Way and retrace your footsteps to your car. Stop, if you wish, at Tablehurst Farm Cafe.

A Search for the Dragon of St Leonard's Forest

14.5km/9miles

Woodland paths through a historic forest, satisfying sections of the High Weald Landscape Trail and enough uphill gradients to walk off a pub lunch.

Leechpool Wood, Horsham » High Weald Landscape Trail » St Leonard's Forest » The Dragon » Blindman's Wood » HWLT » Scragged Oak Hill » Leechpool Wood

Start

Leechpool and Owlbeech Woods free car park, off B2195 Harwood Road, Horsham. GR: TQ 193313.

The Walk

'And there in a vast and unfrequented Place, heathie, vaultie, full of wholesome Shades, and overgrowne Hollowes, where this Serpent is thought to be bred ... '

This is one of my favourite routes, made up of mainly tranquil woodland paths and a rewarding stretch of the High Weald Landscape Trail; look out for the emblem. Climbs go unnoticed because gradients are slow and steady. Stretches of footpath may be boggy so stout shoes are highly recommended.

We begin at Leechpool, a large and ancient woodland. Leave behind the picnic tables and marked walks to venture further afield: and you never know what you might see! The iron industry thrived in the High Weald; around Point 4, look out for mine pits, dug to extract the iron ore from beneath the ground. Amid the trees, deer may surprise you with their quiet presence, and the whisper of leaves triumphs over distant traffic noise.

And what of strange beasts? The dragon or serpent of St Leonard's Forest can be traced to a 1614 illustrated London pamphlet, under the names of John Steele, Christopher Holder and a Widow Woman who dwelled near Faygate. The beast who is rumoured to be around nine feet in length, and with a white ring of scales around its neck, grows fat on rabbits from the great warren but is also thought to have done away with two large 'mastive dogs'. If we believe the fate of one poisoned 17th-century couple, who did not live to bear witness to their own 'woefull Experience', it's been known to spit venom quite some distance so let's hope the dragon you're most likely to see is the pub where you can rest in the safety and comfort of their large garden.

A SEARCH FOR THE DRAGON OF ST LEONARD'S FOREST

DISTANCE: 14.5KM/9MILES » **TOTAL ASCENT**: 290M/951FT » **START GR**: TQ 193313 » **TIME**: ALLOW 4 HOURS PLUS STOPS » **SATNAV**: RH13 6SG » **MAP**: OS EXPLORER OL34, CRAWLEY & HORSHAM, 1:25,000 » **REFRESHMENTS**: THE DRAGON, COLGATE » **NAVIGATION**: GENERALLY STRAIGHTFORWARD ON MAINLY WELL-ESTABLISHED BRIDLEWAYS AND PATHS.

Directions – A Search for the Dragon of St Leonard's Forest

➊ Walk to the entrance of the car park. A footpath starts on the road about 10m south of the entrance but a path cuts through to it. Walk along this signed footpath. Go down a slope. Walk **straight ahead** across a footbridge and up some steps, joining Riverside Walk as it turns right. Follow the dried-up or otherwise streambed along a mud track then walk along a boardwalk.

2 Reach a lane. **Turn left** along the signed bridleway. Occasional cars! **Turn right** along the bridleway at the signpost by St Leonard's Park house, leaving the tarmac path. Walk **straight ahead** past a footpath.

3 Just after the gate, **walk left** on the signed public footpath until you reach the end of a field. Walk **straight ahead** on the fenced footpath which can be muddy. At the end, walk **straight ahead** on the signed footpath passing through a kissing gate on a path through a clearing where motocross race meetings may be held. Soon, **walk right**, leaving this track to pass a wooden waymarker signpost and continue on along the edge of the field. In the corner, pass a currently broken signpost and walk on down the hill.

Continue **straight ahead** at the signpost by the pond, staying on the HWLT. Walk **straight on** past a marker post on this wide track through a forest with Scots pines on your left. Climb a gradual slope and, at the next marker post, **veer left** on a track which narrows. Walk **straight ahead** at the signpost, staying on the HWLT. Pass another signpost amid the bracken clearing and walk **straight ahead**.

4 **Walk left** at the four-way signpost along the bridleway and forest track. Pass a marker post. The track curves right. Stop to look at a Forestry Commission noticeboard. At this path junction, keep walking **straight ahead** along the signed bridleway. Step over a vehicle barrier, pass a bungalow (Ranger's Lodge Wildlife Hospital) and White Heron's Farm. Upon reaching the busy road, **turn right** and walk along the verge.

03 A SEARCH FOR THE DRAGON OF ST LEONARD'S FOREST

Directions – A Search for the Dragon of St Leonard's Forest continued...

5 Cross the lane to have refreshments in The Dragon if you wish. Otherwise, **turn right** down Springfield Lane. At the signpost, leave the lane to **walk a few steps left** then, almost immediately, **turn right** at a second signpost following the signed footpath along a fence. Walk down a fenced rocky section and along a planked section across a bog. Pass a pond. At the fence corner and obscured signpost, **walk right** along the path and planks. Pass another signpost and **walk left** on the footpath heading away from the fence. Cross a footbridge over an idyllic stream with fern-covered banks. **Careful** to stay on the footpath: notices warn this is private land with shooting! Climb over a stile and walk on past a marker post through a bracken-covered heath. Go through a kissing gate. **Walk left** on the signed footpath.

6 **Turn right** along the rough-surfaced lane, following the signed public footpath. **Turn left** at the signpost by Spring Farm and walk along a fenced track. Go through a gate and walk along the edge of a field on the signed footpath. **Turn right** along the lane (occasional traffic!). Pass Lower Grouse Farm and Birchwood.

7 **Turn left** at the signpost: climb over the stile to walk along the hedged footpath with lovely views up to the ridge. At the end of the fence, walk along the footpath and pass two signposts, turning **right** and then **left** to head towards the bottom of the field. Walk **straight ahead** through the copse, a High Weald 'shaw' if ever I saw one. Cross a footbridge over a stream, go up some steps and climb over a stile. Follow the signed footpath **diagonally right** across the grazing field. Pass a signpost. Climb over a stile and **turn left** to walk along the fenced edge of the grazing field and up the hill. Climb over the stile and **turn right** along the signed public footpath through the next field. (There is a well-trodden track leading right along the top of the current field you're in which cuts through to the same bridleway but this is not the right of way.)

8 Look out for the HWLT emblem by the stile. **Turn right** along the fenced bridleway and walk down the hill. Go through a gate and follow the signed bridleway **straight ahead** through the woods. Pass another signpost and walk **straight on** following the HWLT bridleway. Cross the footbridge over the ford. Climb the slope and **turn left** to follow the signed bridleway across a field. **Turn right** at the signpost, and walk along the track, on this side of the gate and adjacent to the fence.

9 Cross the road. Walk **straight on** along the public footpath and through the woods. Cross the footbridge and climb a slow steady track. **Turn left** along the footpath.

10 Cross the forest track and walk a few steps **right**. **Turn left** and follow the signed footpath. Walk **straight ahead** at two more signposts and continue on this woodland track. Pass another signpost and continue across a track and **straight ahead** past yet another signpost to walk down the hill. Cross a wide track and continue down the hill along the signed footpath. Cross the stream at the rocky ford and **turn right** up the footpath. Cross a footbridge and continue.

11 **Turn left** back along this familiar section of the HWLT. Reach the clearing where occasional race meetings are held. Walk on back through the gate and **straight ahead** along the fenced path. Walk back along the field, past the stile. **Turn right** along the signed bridleway.

12 **Turn left** along the signed footpath to walk along the boardwalk. Pass a lake. Go past a signpost and stile and through a copse. Pass another rather atmospheric lake. **Turn right** at the signpost to walk a few steps up. At the second signpost, **turn left**. Pass a marker post. Cross a footbridge and pass another marker post. Walk **straight ahead** at the next three signposts, following the track. Walk across two plank bridges. Follow the track past another sign as the track wends through the trees. Pass a marker post. At the bridleway, **turn right**.

13 You are back at Point 2. **Turn left** along the footpath back to the car park.

OUSE VALLEY VIADUCT

A Village Green & the Ouse Valley Viaduct

16.4km/10.2miles

This satisfying, fast-paced walk works well with a pub stop or a picnic on the green at Staplefield and is a good way to appreciate the splendour of the Ouse Valley Viaduct.

Ardingly Reservoir » Borde Hill » High Weald Landscape Trail » Brook Street » Staplefield » Ouse Valley Viaduct » Ardingly Reservoir

Start

Ardingly Reservoir (paid) car park.
GR: TQ 335286.

The Walk

The walk begins with a pleasant stretch of the High Weald Landscape Trail. The first couple of fields may contain cattle; please see our introductory section (page xiv) for advice on walking near cows. Pleasant woodland paths and agricultural tracks combine with occasional grassy stretches. The bridleway passes through Borde Hill parkland. Divert into the formal gardens, cafe or buy an ice cream.

This route involves some gentle climbing but you're rewarded with sudden vistas over open farmland. Staplefield is probably the best place to stop for lunch. A short walk across the archetypal village green takes you to The Jolly Tanners: a friendly real-ale pub with a lovely garden. Pies are one of their speciality home-cooked offerings. Our route goes past The Victory Inn where tables overlook the green and, as well as the usual fare, you can buy ice lollies all day.

On our return to Ardingly from Staplefield, we follow a small section of the 42-mile Sussex Ouse Valley Way which roughly follows the course of the River Ouse from near its source at Lower Beeding to the coast at Seaford Bay. The Ouse Valley Viaduct is best appreciated at the end of a long walk: its scale, relationship to the High Weald landscape and the sheer audacity of its design all work together and impress! You've probably travelled over it on the London to Brighton train line. Also known as the Balcombe Viaduct, this feat of engineering was opened in 1841 and used 11 million bricks. Thanks to grants from the Railway Heritage Trust and English Heritage, in around 1996 it was restored using matching bricks and around 110 trains pass over this grade-II listed building every day.

A VILLAGE GREEN & THE OUSE VALLEY VIADUCT

DISTANCE: 16.4KM/10.2MILES » **TOTAL ASCENT**: 247M/810FT » **START GR**: TQ 335286 » **TIME**: 4 HOURS PLUS STOPS
SATNAV: RH17 6SQ » **MAP**: OS EXPLORERS OL34, CRAWLEY & HORSHAM AND 135 ASHDOWN FOREST, 1:25,000
REFRESHMENTS: THE JOLLY TANNERS AND THE VICTORY INN, STAPLEFIELD; BORDE HILL CAFES AND ICE CREAMS; PICNIC TABLES BY RESERVOIR » **NAVIGATION**: STRAIGHTFORWARD. ROAD STRETCH ALONG COPYHOLD LANE.

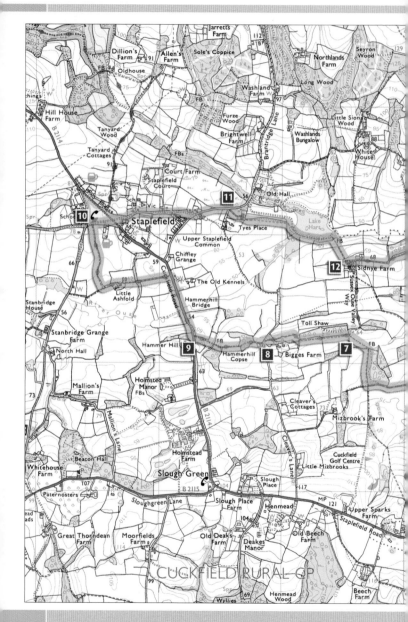

04 **A VILLAGE GREEN & THE OUSE VALLEY VIADUCT**

Directions – A Village Green & the Ouse Valley Viaduct

⊙➤ Walk back out past the car park entrance/ticket machine and, by the waymarker signposts, **turn right** through the metal gates. Walk up the slope on the tarmac road until you reach the metal gate to the left of the sailing club entrance. Pass to the right of the metal gate and walk along a mud or grassy track to the wooden signpost. **Turn left** on the High Weald Landscape Trail (HWLT) towards the wooden gate. To the left of the wooden gate there is a kissing gate. Go through this and walk **straight ahead** along the waymarked footpath. Walk along the fence and through a gap. **Turn left** and, in the corner, walk across the footbridge and follow the signed footpath **straight ahead**. Go across another footbridge.

2 This is the point you return to later. Walk **slightly diagonally right** towards the kissing gate. By the signpost, go through a kissing gate and walk **straight ahead** along a pleasant footpath. Look out for occasional HWLT marker posts and continue on through the woodland on this obvious path. Go through a kissing gate.

3 Walk **straight ahead** along the signed stony footpath. Walk across the railway bridge and follow the signed footpath between some buildings. Go through a kissing gate and follow the track **straight ahead** along the fence. Cross a footbridge and walk **straight ahead**. Go through a gate, across a small footbridge, past a marker post and follow a footpath **straight ahead**. Pass a kissing gate and walk on through the woods.

4 **Turn right** along the road (**caution**: no verge!) following the HWLT. Pass Copyhold Hollow and Bective. Cross a railway bridge and pass some cottages on this road stretch of the HWLT. **Turn left** at the end of Copyhold Lane for a short distance.

5 **Turn right** along the signed bridleway through Borde Hill. Walk straight on past the roundabout, past the entrance and **straight ahead** along the track beside the fence. Go through a gate and walk on through Borde Hill grazing fields. At the junction, walk through the gate following the HWLT along a signed footpath through a field. Walk across the ridge, enjoying fine views over the Weald. Cross a stile and walk **very slightly right** following the signed footpath down and along the edge of the trees. Cross a stile. Walk on and cross another stile and follow the footpath **straight ahead**. Pass the signpost and head **straight ahead** along a fence. Cross a footbridge and a stile and follow the path on through the woods and up the side of a field through Tanyard Farm. Follow the path right by the signpost through ferns and over a stile. **Walk left**, passing another signpost, and down a small slope. **Walk left** before the building, following the footpath along the fence and up past a timber building. The path is hedged and then continues past the Chapel Gallery to the road.

6 Cross the road and **walk right** a short distance. **Turn left** along the signed bridleway (Sparks Lane) opposite the *Brook Street* sign. Walk **straight ahead** on the bridleway at Lower Sparks Farm. This narrowish path carries on through a woodland. **Turn right** along the signed footpath at a wide gate and path crossroads. Walk along the fence and go through a wooden gate and then a metal gate. Follow the signed footpath **diagonally left** across the field. Go through a metal gate.

7 **Walk left** following the public footpath across the track, through another gate and along the edge of a field. Go through a gap into another field. Cross a stile and **walk right** a short way. Go through a gate and **walk left** along the signed footpath. Far-reaching views to the right. At the signpost, **go left** through the gate, through an opening and **turn right** at the signpost along the tarmac drive and public footpath.

8 **Turn right** along the signed footpath before Garden Cottage. This old stony track runs through woods. Go through a gate and follow the signed footpath along the edge of a field. Go through a gate and walk on along the track.

9 **Turn right** along (busy!) Cuckfield Road and walk on the rough verge where possible. **Turn left** along the signed bridleway to Little Ashfold Farm. Pass a house and sign-post and leave the concrete track to walk **straight ahead** on the grassy footpath. Pass another sign. **Turn right** at the three-way signpost and walk through a kissing gate. Walk along the edge of a crop field and on past a marker post to a road.

10 This is Staplefield. **Turn right**, passing The Victory Inn. Cross the main road and walk **straight ahead** along the lane. Pass St Mark's church and school and later some cottages. **Walk straight ahead** at the white signpost towards Balcombe.

Directions – A Village Green & the Ouse Valley Viaduct continued...

11 **Turn right** at the signpost and follow the public footpath. At the signpost, follow the path to the **left**, staying on the tarmac track. Follow the public footpath through a private garden. Afterwards, **turn left** at the sign and walk along the edge of a crop field. At the signpost, **turn slightly left** into the woods, so that initially you keep going in roughly the same direction. The path soon bends right and along a fence. The path goes through a linear copse or wood and runs alongside a stream for a while. **Turn right** at the signpost, across the footbridge and walk up the fenced path and slope. Go through a gate and walk on along the path.

12 Go through a gate and **walk diagonally left** through Sidnye Farm. **Turn left** at the three-way signpost in the middle of the buildings. Walk between two barns and **turn left** and **then right**. Walk past tile-hung red houses and continue along the track, enjoying some pleasant views over farmland.

13 **Turn right** along the minor road. At a busy road, **cross**, **turn left** briefly and **turn right** at the sign. Walk along a track. Pass some corrugated barns on this long stretch of tarmac path. The track curves towards some buildings. **Turn left** at the signpost, within sight of Great Bentley Farm, going through a metal gate and down some steps. Walk along the right-hand edge of a field along the footpath. Where the boundary curves, see a sign beneath a tree. Continue on and cross a footbridge. Walk **diagonally right** following the waymarked footpath. Spot the Ouse Valley Viaduct on your right. Go through a gate halfway along the top edge and follow the signed footpath and Sussex Ouse Valley Way **diagonally right** up the slope. Cross a couple of cramped stiles and follow the footpath **straight ahead** towards Ryelands Farm. Walk through a kissing gate and past a waymarked marker post, following the footpath **straight ahead** through the buildings. After the farm, **turn left** along the drive towards the tunnel but, almost immediately, look for the marker post on your **right** and follow the footpath through a kissing gate. Enjoy the architectural splendour of the viaduct. Walk **diagonally left** to the far corner and through a couple of kissing gates. Walk beneath the viaduct and on through a small kissing gate. Cross the road. **Walk right** a short distance past the buildings and across the bridge.

14 Turn left at the signpost through a kissing gate and walk along the footpath which follows an overgrown stream for some way. Go through a gate and **straight on** along a mud track. Walk past Balcombe estate.

15 Reach the point where the path forked earlier in your walk. **Head left** towards the footbridge. Cross the stream and walk **slightly diagonally right** and across the next footbridge. **Walk straight up** the slope and **turn right** through the gap and back round and through the next kissing gate. Arrive back at Ardingly Reservoir.

HIGH WEALD CROP FIELDS

THE WALK OF MANY LAST CLIMBS: BALCOMBE LAKE & ARDINGLY RESERVOIR

DISTANCE: 19.8KM/12.3MILES » **TOTAL ASCENT**: 505M/1,656FT » **START GR**: TQ 366325 » **TIME**: ALLOW 5–5.5 HOURS PLUS STOPS » **SATNAV**: RH19 4PN » **MAP**: OS EXPLORER 135, ASHDOWN FOREST, 1:25,000 » **REFRESHMENTS**: THE HALF MOON INN, BALCOMBE; PICNIC TABLES OR OCCASIONAL SAILING CLUB SNACK KIOSK, ARDINGLY RESERVOIR; THE ARDINGLY INN AND FELLOWS BAKERY, ARDINGLY (CLOSES 1 P.M. ON SATURDAYS); THE CAT INN, WEST HOATHLY » **NAVIGATION**: GENERALLY STRAIGHTFORWARD BUT WATCH OUT FOR EASY-TO-MISS TURNS.

The Walk of Many Last Climbs: Balcombe Lake & Ardingly Reservoir

19.8km/12.3miles

Easy bridleways and glittering waterside paths are interspersed with climbs through rolling Weald and woodland valleys on this challenging walk.

West Hoathly » Chiddinglye » Balcombe Lake » Great Burrow Wood » Ardingly Reservoir » Ardingly » High Weald Landscape Trail » West Hoathly

Start

Finche Field free car park, West Hoathly. GR: TQ 366325.

The Walk

Your path threads its way through wide-open agricultural countryside which later descends into peaceful woodland. As you approach Balcombe Pond, a planked walkway leads over a marsh and, in season, the water draws an abundance of damselflies and runs on down the forested valley towards Balcombe Lake. Local farm buildings date as far back as the early 15th century and it's not hard to imagine why settlers would thrive here. Soak up some reflected sunshine as you walk around Ardingly Reservoir: light flickers on the water, birds call, fish splash. Great Burrow Wood gives you a feel for the woodland valley that existed before the reservoir was built. Kingfishers and great crested grebe are known to nest here. Why not seek out the bird hide in the nature reserve?

After a meander through Ardingly, the High Weald Landscape Trail becomes spectacular; its wooded gills and Wealden streams suggest a sense of hidden drama. The name of Fulling Mill Farm gives a clue to past local industries, since 'fulling' is a process which follows weaving. Before the 11th century, a walker 'trod' the cloth, and later, water power mechanised the process. All this will distract you from the climbs: they're worth it though, for uplifting views of patchwork fields, shimmering lakes and woods that whisper tales of the past.

Picturesque West Hoathly feels tucked away but has it always been a haven? Drop into The Priest House to have a potter around this interesting 15th-century Wealden hall house, now furnished with country furniture and domestic objects which give a good sense of how people used to live. Picnics are permitted in the cottage garden, a veritable source of culinary, medicinal and household herbs. St Margaret's church is worth exploring too; the churchyard rewards with far-reaching views over Sussex and, inside, on the south wall, look out for a plaque to Ann Tree, a local woman listed as Mother Tree in *Foxe's Book of Martyrs*, and burned to death for her Protestant beliefs during Mary Tudor's reign. On a lighter note, you may wish to end your day with welcome refreshments at The Cat Inn, a friendly 16th-century free house.

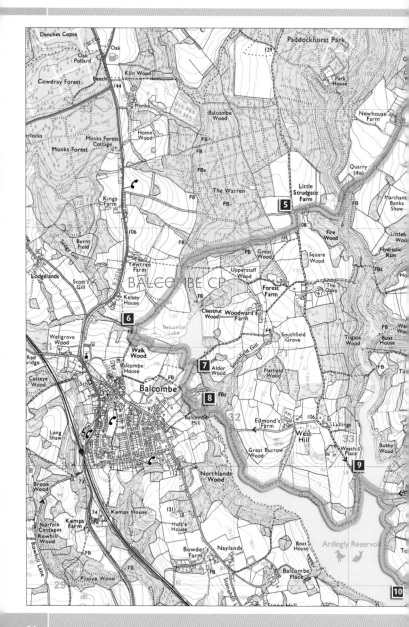

05 THE WALK OF MANY LAST CLIMBS: BALCOMBE LAKE & ARDINGLY RESERVOIR

Directions – The Walk of Many Last Climbs: Balcombe Lake & Ardingly Reservoir

⊙ **Turn right** following the tarmac path out of the car park. At the signpost and toposcope, walk **straight ahead** along the footpath. At the second signpost, continue **straight ahead** along the residential road. At the end of Sandy Lane, **turn left** along the lane.

2 **Turn right** along the signed public footpath opposite The Cat Inn. Walk along this grassy path and over a stile. **Continue** onwards. Pass a waymarked post and continue **straight ahead** along the hedge. Pass another signpost. Keep walking **straight ahead** where the footpath joins a stony track and then concrete lane. Pass Garden and Vine cottages and then Chiddinglye house.

3 Walk **diagonally right** at the junction and signpost. Soon pass another waymarked signpost and walk **straight ahead**, staying on this track. Follow the signposted footpath through the kissing gate and continue through a Wealden wood interspersed with rocks. Cross a stile and **walk left**. Follow the footpath round the edge of the grazing field along and round to the right. Cross a stile and footbridge following the signed footpath through some woods. At the signpost, **turn left** and cross an old bridge over a stream. Walk along an overgrown narrow section. Reach the road.

4 Walk **right**, and then **left** along the signed public footpath through Old House estate. Pass between two ponds. Pass rugby posts and Old House. **Turn left** at the signpost and walk along the hedged footpath. Go down some steps and over a couple of stiles. Keep **straight ahead** at the signpost. Cross a stile and **walk diagonally left** along the waymarked footpath through the open field. Cross a stile and walk **straight ahead** on the signed footpath. Pass a barn and go through a gate, following the tarmac footpath **straight ahead**. Pass a house and corrugated barn and walk **straight ahead** staying on the signed footpath and long tarmac lane. Pass a lake. Climb a steepish hill and pass a stone barn at Little Strudgate Farm. Cross a stile.

5 **Turn left** along Paddockhurst Lane. **Turn right** along a lane, following an **easy-to-miss** signpost, submerged in ferns. Pass some houses and go through a gate. Pass through Wealden woods on this 'cobbled' track. Pass a marker post and walk **straight ahead**. At the signpost, continue **straight ahead**, staying on your footpath. Cross a stone bridge and walk past another signpost, keeping **straight ahead**. Go through a gate and follow the signed footpath **straight ahead**. Pass a marker post.

6 **Turn left** at the three-way signpost, down several steps and then **right** along a marvellously long planked walkway through a marshy area. Climb up some steps and a slope. **Turn left** at the signpost along the undulating mud track. Follow this curving footpath through the woods to a signpost. **Turn right** and walk across several footbridges. Follow the footpath along the edge of Balcombe Lake and through a kissing gate. Walk along the edge of a field. Cross a footbridge and go through a kissing gate. Walk **diagonally left** along the signed footpath. Go through another kissing gate.

7 Walk **right** and follow the signed footpath along the lane (occasional fast traffic). Climb the hill! At the top, **go left** for a short distance about 50m along the road. **Turn right** along the signed bridleway and, almost immediately, **follow the bridleway left** at the marker post through a wood. Continue past a signpost. Go through a gate and **walk left** a few metres on the signed footpath through the grazing field. Go through a kissing gate and **take care** down the many steps.

8 **Walk right** along the road and across the reservoir bridge. Walk up the hill. **Turn right** along the bridleway. This runs along the edge of Ardingly Reservoir. At the end, go through a gate to a road.

9 **Turn right** along the roadside path. At the signpost, **turn right** and go through a gate to walk along the side of the reservoir. Pass a stile by a signpost and continue along this glittering waterside path. Walk almost to the end.

Directions – The Walk of Many Last Climbs: Balcombe Lake & Ardingly Reservoir continued…

10 **Turn left** at the signpost by the noticeboard and wooded area. Climb over the stile and leave the reservoir to walk up the right-hand side of the field and through a gap in the corner. Continue **straight ahead** towards a metal gate. It's a steep climb but worth it for the views back over the reservoir. You are at Townhouse Farm. See a four-way signpost and walk **straight ahead** along the lane, which becomes gradually more residential. Pass a marker post and continue **straight ahead**. At the next signpost, walk **straight on** along the lane.

11 At the signpost, leave the footpath to walk along the public lane. By St Peter's church, **turn right** towards Ardingly village. Walk along Street Lane, using the pavement where possible. Pass St Peter's school. Keep going along this lane past a footpath and Holmans (a road). Pass Oaklands and walk to the end, where you will find Fellows bakery and The Ardingly Inn. By the pub, **turn left** and **left again** along High Street. You need to cross over before the post office and antiques shop.

12 **Turn right** along the twitten where the sign on the house says *High Street 28–60 even no's only*. Go through a kissing gate and walk ahead along the signed footpath, heading **slightly left** across the field to another signpost by the gap beside the hedge. Continue **straight ahead** over a stile and along the footpath. Enjoy far-reaching views as you descend this grassy field. In the bottom right corner climb over a high stile and walk down the footpath beside the fence. Go through a gate and walk **diagonally left** past the house as waymarked on the signpost. **Ignore** another three-way signpost to your right as it's confusing, but head for the bottom left corner where you should see a signpost in the fence. Walk down the footpath into the woods and follow the path round to the right.

At the next signpost, **walk left** and across a footbridge over a stream. Follow the signed footpath **straight ahead** through an amazing meadow teeming with wildlife. Cross a stile and walk **straight ahead**, following the waymarked High Weald Landscape Trail (HWLT). Climb a steep grassy hill, cross another stile and walk on and up the slope. By a house, cross a stile and walk on following the footpath past a low barn and up a hill. **Walk straight ahead** at the signpost up this sometimes rock-lined sunken lane and footpath.

13 At the lane, **walk right** up the hill. Pass Ludwell house. **Turn left** at the signpost along the fenced footpath and walk along the hedge. Go through a wide gate and follow the footpath **straight ahead** through Hook Farm Campsite's grassy field. Head for a gate in the corner of the trees and follow the signposted footpath **straight ahead** into the woods. Go down and across a footbridge. **Keep left** and climb the slope. At the top, reach a clearing and a signpost. **Turn right** along the track. Soon, **keep left** at the fork, passing the bridleway marker post. The path runs along the top of wooded valley. Pass the gates and continue **straight on** along the bridleway. Climb a long steep hill above a stream.

14 At the top, **turn right**, staying on this track. Walk between Philpots Manor School buildings. **Turn left** and **left again** along the signed bridleway. Pass a quarry. Climb a long steady hill.

15 **Walk left** along the lane into West Hoathly. Pass the Priest House and the Manor House. Pass St Margaret's church. Walk **straight ahead** past The Cat Inn and **right** back along Sandy Lane to the car park.

BALCOMBE LAKE

SECTION 2

The Heart of the High Weald

Ashdown Forest offers the largest area of open access land in the South East. This mixture of heathland and woodland is made unique by its common land usage over the centuries and is also celebrated for its association with A.A. Milne and his creation Winnie the Pooh. In these walks I have chosen to explore woodland at the fringes of the Ashdown Forest. Let a sunken lane lead you upwards and, from the ridge, admire the seasonal shades and varied textures of mixed woodland and fields. As we move east, the landscape seems to become less populated and many of these walks lead you to rare tucked-away habitats: steep-sided wooded valleys or gills, rocky outcrops, restored heathland and floodplain. Train buffs will enjoy some railway nostalgia, evident in a puff of steam and an echoing whistle. There is much to enjoy here.

RESTORED HEATHLAND AT RSPB BROADWATER WARREN (ROUTE 7)

TAKE THE HIGH WEALD TRAIL TO HARTFIELD

DISTANCE: 12.9KM/8MILES » **TOTAL ASCENT**: 145M/475FT » **START GR**: TQ 426350 » **TIME**: ALLOW 3 HOURS PLUS STOPS » **SATNAV**: RH18 5HE » **MAP**: OS EXPLORER 135, ASHDOWN FOREST, 1:25,000 » **REFRESHMENTS**: TABLEHURST FARM CAFE, ON FOREST WAY; PIGLETS TEAROOM IN POOH CORNER, THE ANCHOR INN AND THE VILLAGE STORES, ALL ON HARTFIELD'S HIGH STREET; VARIOUS OPTIONS IN FOREST ROW INCLUDING TAFFELS CAFE (RECOMMENDED) » **NAVIGATION**: GENERALLY STRAIGHTFORWARD AND MADE EASIER BY USING DIRECTIONS IN CONJUNCTION WITH HWLT MARKER POSTS. TAKE CARE AT THE CAMPSITE.

VIEWS FROM THE HIGH WEALD LANDSCAPE TRAIL

06 Take the High Weald Trail to Hartfield

12.9km/8miles

A tranquil meander through grazing meadows, pasture and woodland with a chance to explore A.A. Milne's home village of Hartfield and an easy return on Forest Way.

Forest Row » Forest Way » High Weald Landscape Trail » Cansiron Lane » Paupersdale Wood » Hartfield » Forest Way » Forest Row

Start

Lower Road car park, off Station Road. Free parking in long- and medium-stay bays. GR: TQ 426350. Alternative: Hartfield Road Car Park with public toilets if community centre open.

The Walk

This northerly section of the High Weald Landscape Trail feels tranquil but its well-trodden paths tend to be well established, although one or two of the narrower tracks can be a little overgrown. Look out for the distinctive silver and green High Weald Landscape Trail emblems to guide you on your way. This landscape is so typical of the High Weald: rolling hills, shaws, crop fields, grazing meadow and grasslands.

The initial stretch involves a gradual climb but the path is so intriguing; take your time. This could well be an old sunken lane, used for centuries and shared with badgers, foxes and rabbits. As you emerge on to Cansiron Lane, you are rewarded with views over the Ashdown Forest. Continue through grazing fields and enjoy expansive views over the valley where you can see the small woods or shaws that cling to the edges

of irregular, mainly grazing, fields. Paupersdale Wood is used for rearing pheasants but may also yield the scent of bluebells or a display of butterflies in flight.

In this walk, you can enjoy views over the Ashdown Forest immortalised by A.A. Milne as the 'enchanted places' of 'Pooh Corner'. Alexander Milne lived at a farmhouse near Hartfield and would quite possibly have walked though this landscape. The illustrations by E.H. Shepard are equally influential on our psyche and capture the essence of our High Weald forests, heath, streams and rolling fields.

After refreshments in Hartfield, enjoy a dander back along the old railway line and linear country park, Forest Way. Look out for alder and willow trees as this old railway line runs through the River Medway floodplain. If you wish to pause awhile to enjoy the wildlife, there are occasional benches and picnic tables, or take advantage of the easy walking surface to enjoy a fast pace. The straightforward return makes this walk tempting for those who like an obvious route home.

06 TAKE THE HIGH WEALD TRAIL TO HARTFIELD

Directions – Take the High Weald Trail to Hartfield

⑤➤ Leave the car park through the metal bike barriers and cross Station Road to join the bridleway at the wooden waymarker. Follow the path through a children's play area. At the second bench, **turn left** passing the skateboard ramps to walk along a tree-lined mud track. At the three-way wooden waymarker **turn left** along the bridleway. Keep **straight ahead** at the next wooden signpost staying on the bridleway to cross the bridge. Upon joining Forest Way, **turn left** towards East Grinstead. Take the **right-hand track** as signed on the small blue National Cycle Network 21 arrow on the post which soon ascends to a tarmac lane.

2 **Turn right** at signs for Tablehurst Farm. Walk round **left** past a barn and on through a metal gate with a High Weald Landscape Trail (HWLT) emblem on the marker post. Follow this part-concrete track round. Pass a couple of barely noticeable marker posts set back into hedges. Then, at an obvious marker post by a wide metal gate, **turn left** to follow the HWLT along the narrow wooded track parallel to the field. Pass a storage area and keep **straight ahead** through an HWLT waymarked walkers' stile beside a metal gate. Walk up and to the right of the enclosure to cross the stile in the top corner. Follow the trail **diagonally left** on the track. Go **straight ahead** at the field end, passing an HWLT marker post. After about 50m look out for an **easy-to-miss** small and overgrown path; **branch right** at this unsigned fork and climb a slight slope on this intriguing track. Is this an old sunken lane? At the top, cross the stile at the waymarker sign and follow the footpath **straight ahead** on this wooded track. See a house out in the meadow. Pass a marker post and cross a stile.

3 **Turn right** along Cansiron Lane, enjoying views over the Ashdown Forest. Pass Blackberry Hill Farmhouse and occasional houses. At the junction, see the marker post and cross the stile. Walk **diagonally left** on the HWLT though the grazing field and cross the stile to enjoy far-reaching views. Walk a few steps to the end of the fence where a marker post may be visible in the hedge. Keep walking **straight ahead** on the HWLT down towards the corner. Cross the stile into the woodland, following the HWLT emblem. Cross a plank bridge. Pass a marker post. Reach an open field and another marker post. Follow the HWLT **straight ahead** along the edge of the crop field, which may be rich in grassland flowers. You may hear a distant steam train. Pass the marker post and gate and walk **straight ahead** through the next field. Pass another marker post and walk **straight ahead** through the next field.

4 At the signpost junction follow the HWLT **straight ahead**. Go over the stile and follow the HWLT through the campsite, although it may not be obvious the field is used as such. Take care here: pass a lake but, before the track curves right, walk **straight ahead** across the grass. Cross the mud track and, with the lake behind you, look for a narrow path, running through the middle of the field ahead of you. Take this path.

5 Cross the tarmac path and follow the waymarked HWLT over the stile and through the 'opening' fence. Walk **diagonally left** across the field. Cross the stile and walk **diagonally right** across the pasture, keeping in the same direction. Cross the **left-hand stile** in the corner (there are two!), being sure to follow the HWLT. **Walk right** along the fence and across the planks and on through the woods. Cross a stile and walk **straight ahead** across the field and then climb over another stile and walk **straight ahead** across another grazing field. Cross another stile and follow the HWLT **straight ahead** through the middle of a crop field. See Hartfield church spire ahead. At the waymarker, walk **straight ahead** past the redundant stile, staying on the HWLT. Cross the stream on the footbridge and then a stile.

6 **Turn left** along Forest Way to enjoy a short loop to Hartfield. (To return directly to Forest Row **turn right** instead.) Pass beneath a bridge and immediately **turn left** and up the embankment to leave Forest Way. **Walk left** across the bridge and through the gate along the grassy bridleway. In the corner, there are three gateways and an opening. To stay on your waymarked bridleway, go through the **third gate** and walk **straight ahead**. Pass through a gateway and walk **straight on** past the pavilion community building and recreation ground. At the road, **turn right**. Explore the High Street or return to Forest Way along the HWLT which leaves Hartfield by the gate **on the other side of the park**. Walk past the marker posts beside the tennis courts. Climb over the stile and follow the path. Walk past several waymarked fences and over a stile.

Turn left to walk approx. 5km back to the start along Forest Way. You will pass the odd bench or picnic table. Pass some houses and then some allotments. Leave Forest Way where you joined it and **turn left** to retrace your steps to the start.

ERIDGE ROCKS, SUSSEX WILDLIFE TRUST NATURE RESERVE

07 Rocks, Railway & Heath

12.9km/8miles

A delightful walk through nature reserves that puts life into perspective: enjoy spectacular sandstone outcrops, wonderful heathland and the nostalgia of a steam railway.

Groombridge » Birchden Wood » Harrison's Rocks » Park Corner » High Weald Landscape Trail » Eridge Rocks » Broadwater Warren » Groombridge Place » Groombridge

Start

Groombridge Memorial Hall car park, Station Road. Roadside, if full.
GR: TQ 531373.

The Walk

Our walk starts near Groombridge Spa Valley Railway Station, so steam engine enthusiasts could combine a train journey with our trail or simply appreciate trains from nearby footpaths. This route passes two Cretaceous rocky outcrops, formed by the hardest edges of High Weald sandstone. The first crag, Harrison's Rocks, is popular with climbers while any otherworldly familiarity may stem from a 1981 *Dr Who* episode. The second, Eridge Rocks, is a superb nature reserve, rescued by Sussex Wildlife Trust. Nestling amidst veteran trees, these magnificent 135-million-year-old rocks will take you aback with their scale and the community of plants they support: rare mosses, liverworts and ferns thrive here. The textured surface of these huge boulders is rich in beauty and has borne witness to Mesolithic-struck flints, Romano-British smelting, the 17th-century discovery of the 'Tunbridge filmy-fern' and elaborately costumed Victorian dinner parties.

Broadwater Warren will amaze too, and not just with its appealing viewpoints. The RSPB is restoring this former conifer plantation to a historic landscape more characteristic of the High Weald: a patchwork of precious heath, native trees and scrub with clumps of pines and rare woodland mire or boggy sections. When I walk here, I can imagine how a more widespread High Weald landscape might once have appeared; low heathland is increasingly under threat, with over 80% having been lost since 1800. Today, this valuable habitat attracts varied invertebrates, the adder and the dormouse as well as drawing in threatened birds such as nightjar, woodlark, lesser spotted woodpecker, marsh tit and spotted flycatcher, who all breed on site.

ROCKS, RAILWAY & HEATH

DISTANCE: 12.9KM/8MILES » **TOTAL ASCENT**: 193M/633FT » **START GR**: TQ 531373 » **TIME**: ALLOW 3-4 HOURS PLUS STOPS » **SATNAV**: TN3 9QX » **MAP**: OS EXPLORER 135, ASHDOWN FOREST, 1:25,000 » **REFRESHMENTS**: THE JUNCTION INN, STATION ROAD, GROOMBRIDGE. THE NEVILL CREST AND GUN, ERIDGE GREEN » **NAVIGATION**: STRAIGHTFORWARD. FOLLOW THE HEATH AND WOODLAND TRAIL IN RSPB BROADWATER WARREN. PATHS IN BOTH NATURE RESERVES ARE PERMISSIVE AND MAY ALTER: SEE RELEVANT WEBSITES. DOGS ON LEADS AS REQUESTED, DUE TO GROUND-NESTING SPECIES.

Directions — Rocks, Railway & Heath

↱ Cross Station Road to walk up Corseley Road. At the top, walk **straight ahead** past Orchard Rise and a marker post. Pass the church.

2 **Turn left** at the marker post by the school and walk along the footpath. Go through a gate and across a railway bridge over the Spa Valley Railway. Go through the kissing gate and follow the footpath beside some fenced grazing fields. Go through the gate and pass the marker post with the High Weald Landscape Trail (HWLT) emblem. At the next gate, **turn right** along the lane following the HWLT. Go down the hill through Birchden Wood, following the lane as it curves right to the car park (toilets).

3 **Turn left** at the signpost, following the Forest Walk, initially for a few steps past the large noticeboard and through the fence posts. Look carefully to your **right** for a post located close to the ground with a yellow waymarker; follow this mud track, gently descending through the woods. Walk on through a clearing. See the railway tracks to your right. Pass the gate for Harrison's Rocks. Walk **straight ahead** passing the waymarked post. See the rocks on your left. Pass a marker post and more rocky cliffs. Go through a gate and walk on along the fenced path. Pass another gate and a house. Where the track joins a lane, look for the marker post and walk **straight ahead** following the HWLT in front of Forge Farm Oast and Forge Farmhouse. Pass another marker post and walk **straight ahead** along the fenced path. You may spot cobbles beneath your feet or larger rocks in the woods as you walk up through the woods. At the fork, **keep right**. Walk along the hedged path for some time enjoying occasional views over the rolling Weald. Pass a house and climb over a stile and walk **straight ahead** following the waymarked footpath. Pass a farm. Climb slowly along the easy walking hard track. Reach a road.

4 **Turn right** down Eridge Road, following the HWLT as signed on the marker post by the house, Goldsmiths. Walk down the hill. Pass some cottages.

07 ROCKS, RAILWAY & HEATH

5 Turn left at the marker post. Cross the stile and follow the public footpath towards Eridge Green. Pass a marker post and walk across several footbridges over a stream. **Turn right** along the edge of the field for a few steps. **Careful here: turn left** at the marker post with the silver HWLT disc. Walk across the field on the footpath, heading initially slightly right and then straight across the field. To regain the footpath, **turn left** at the grassy crossing place over the ditch currently next to a rusty broken gate and walk along the grass or mud footpath heading to the right of the house and its fence. Walk **straight ahead** along the fence and straight across the field, with a second house on your distant left.

6 Turn right along the lane, noting a waymarker post on the corner. Pass the first Sussex Nature Reserve post and path. **Turn left** at the waymarked signpost into the woods. This mud footpath leads to a lane.

ERIDGE ROCKS

7 **Turn left** along Warren Farm Lane but almost immediately **turn left** again into Eridge Rocks Nature Reserve car park. Walk past the gate and along the path, pausing to admire the life flourishing about this sandstone outcrop. At the fork, **walk left**. Follow the path **straight on** past more huge boulders, enjoying subtle patterns in the rock surfaces. Walk on past more rocks, **ignoring** any offshoot paths. Pass an SWT Eridge Rocks notice-board. Walk **straight on** past a marker post at a rough crossroads of mud tracks.

8 Arrive at the Veteran Oak and noticeboard in RSPB Broadwater Warren reserve. **Walk right** and **look out for green arrows** on marker posts to follow the green Heathland and Woodland Trail: see the RSPB *Finding your way around* map on the noticeboard. Pass Decoy Pond and a sign to *Heathland Viewpoint*. Climb a hill and reach a gate which may have a seasonal sign about wild Exmoor ponies. Go through and walk on. Pass the Nightjar Viewpoint and **walk left** as signed. Pass a notice about military history. Walk on until you **turn left** through a gate. Walk across the car park to continue the Heath and Woodland Trail. **Walk right** and go through a gate as waymarked by the green arrow. Walk onwards, keeping an eye out for regular green arrows as you walk through the distracting beauty of this heathland. Descend a hill and go through a gate then **turn right** along a stream, following the arrow. Go along some walkways and footbridges through the wet woodland. Pass another marker post: you are back on main tracks. Keep walking. Go through another gate and along the fenced track or higher, drier path, which can be accessed a further 50m along the track. Reach a gate on to the road but **walk left** as signed by the green arrow to continue further through the reserve. **Turn right** at the next junction and green arrow. Pass a *Heathland Birds* sign. Reach a gate.

9 You are about to leave the green arrow trail. Go through the gate and walk to the green arrow post on the opposite side of the path. **Ignore** the track you've just crossed and instead **turn right** along a smaller narrow permissive path which is adjacent to a field. Follow this muddy track through the trees with the field to your left. At the end, go through a kissing gate. **Take a few steps right** to reach the very end of Park Corner Lane and stand near the first black and white bollard.

10 **Go straight** across the road and see the stone marker post by the low wall. Walk through the gap and **straight ahead** on the footpath through Birchden Farm. Cross a stile or go through a gate and walk past the oast house on the grassy footpath. Pass the vineyard and house. Pass a marker post and **turn left** to cross a stile. Walk to the **right** to head along the top of the field. Pass some metal farm gates and continue to the far corner. Look out for an **easy-to-miss** unsigned gap where the trodden path leads into the trees. Follow the unmarked path in the same direction. Cross a footbridge and pass a marker post. Follow the footpath **straight ahead**.

11 At the house, walk **straight on** past the first marker post towards the waymarked signpost. **Turn left** along the grassy path, following the signed footpath. Continue past a large pond and follow the edge of the field to walk up the hill. At the end of the hedge, a signpost is perhaps obscured by foliage. Keep walking in the same direction on this footpath across the middle of this wide meadow. Pass through a gap in the hedge and onwards to another gap in the next hedge. Climb over the waymarked stile and walk **straight ahead**.

12 As you near the railway line, cross the next stile and footbridge. **Turn right** across another stile and through the tunnel beneath the steam railway. Cross another stile and walk along the footpath beside the fence. Climb over another stile. Walk along the grassy footpath heading to the left of the red-brick house: this is Groombridge Place.

13 **Turn left** to walk away from the stone bridge on the gravel path. Pass the metal gate and see a waymarked fence and walk **straight ahead** along the grassy fenced foot-path. Follow the footpath (and train signs) round to go through a metal gate and across the park back to the start.

08 A Wild & Woodland Walk Around Mayfield

13km/8.1miles

A pretty walk through open spaces and woodlands; demanding terrain and navigation so allow plenty of time to enjoy these wonderful woodland paths, little used and oh so historic.

Mayfield » Hawksden Park Wood » Hare Holt » Batts Wood » Wadhurst Park » Combe Wood » Coggins Mill » Vicarage Wood » Mayfield

Start
Long-stay free car park on South Street, Mayfield. GR: TQ 587269.

The Walk
'The sweetest village in England,' wrote poet Coventry Patmore, and Mayfield does boast charm and exceptional views over the High Weald. This walk can be idyllic: we once sat on a fallen tree trunk to picnic by a babbling stream beside a sunny glade. However, some paths and woods may feel isolated, there are no refreshment stops and there's a fair bit of climbing on soft ground. You may not see another walker for miles.

Mayfield's tranquil air can be deceptive. Smuggling was widespread. As you walk down Fletching Street, look on the left for a tall house with masonry at its base, then half-timber and brick, then clapperboard. Once known as Smuggler's Cottage, this building was cleverly equipped with two cellars to fool the excisemen.

Surrounding woods may captivate with a quiet beauty but, during the iron industry, the village boomed. Local sand and clay yielded iron ore, the woods provided charcoal, and streams running through gills and valleys harnessed water power for the hammers and bellows of the furnaces and forges. The cannon on the High Street is a clue to what was produced here: during the late 16th century, the Mayfield Foundry was one of the main gun-producing centres in Europe. Hawksden was the site of a forge. The timber-framed hall house by the stone bridge at Point 5 may have once been home to a hammersmith, and Hare Holt was probably the home of an ironmaster. A blast foundry flourished in Vicarage Woods. Imagine the yell of a labourer, the thud of an axe hitting a tree, the smell of burning charcoal or the sting of smoke as you follow the wide stream. Leave the woodland on a stone and brick track which follows what was once the route of the Mayfield to Tunbridge Wells coach road and enjoy the final climb back up to the village.

A WILD & WOODLAND WALK AROUND MAYFIELD

DISTANCE: 13KM/8.1MILES » **TOTAL ASCENT**: 371M/1,218FT » **START GR**: TQ 587269 » **TIME**: ALLOW 4 HOURS PLUS STOPS
SATNAV: TN20 6BE » **MAP**: OS EXPLORER 136, HIGH WEALD, 1:25,000 » **REFRESHMENTS**: PICNIC ADVISED; VARIOUS IN MAYFIELD, INCLUDING THE MIDDLE HOUSE, THE PINK CABBAGE PRODUCE COMPANY, THE ROSE & CROWN » **NAVIGATION**: TRICKY IN SEVERAL WOODLAND SECTIONS. GPS CAN BE PATCHY AND PATHS UNSIGNED.

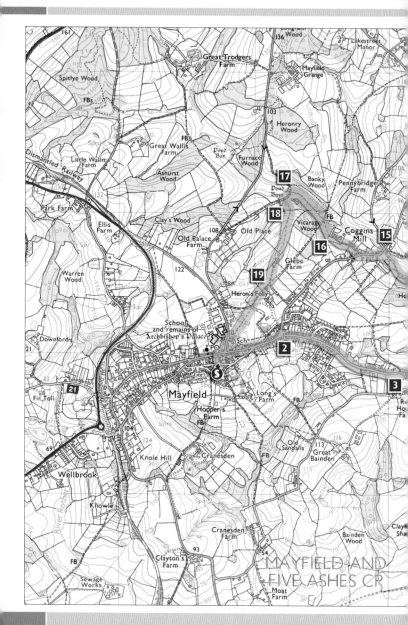

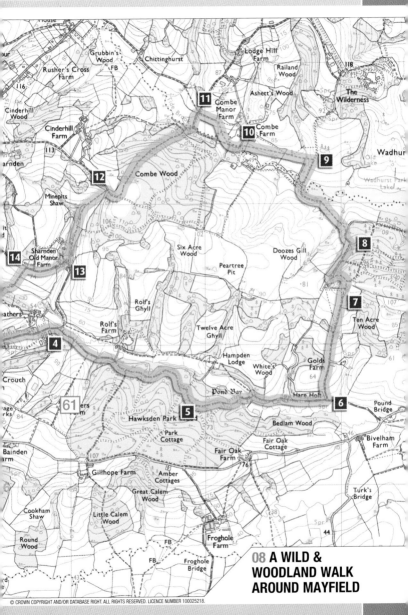

08 A WILD & WOODLAND WALK AROUND MAYFIELD

Directions – A Wild & Woodland Walk Around Mayfield

➲ Go out the main entrance of the car park and walk **straight ahead** up a narrow road, Holders Lane. Emerge on the High Street opposite the Mayfield Cannon. Cross to look and **turn right**. Walk along the High Street and past an old entrance to Mayfield School. At the junction, cross the road and walk **straight ahead** down Fletching Street. Pass The Carpenters Arms and, later, the oast house.

2 Take the **right** fork at the white signpost towards Broad Oak. Walk along East Street for some time, past lots of houses and then along a less residential hedged section. Pass gated Fairlawn Manor and Bay Tree House. **Ignore** both a waymarker post and a walkers' gate on your right. Pass some more houses.

3 **Easy to miss**: leave the lane to walk **left** to follow the bridleway that runs before Stoneycroft house. Walk past the small Wealden Walks waymarked post beside the right-hand stone gatepost for the adjacent private road to Merrieweathers house. Walk on past Stoneycroft and down the hill. Take the **left-hand** waymarked lower fork just before the *Private* sign and outbuilding. Could this be an old sunken lane? See a pond at the farm on your left. At the end of the fence, walk **straight on**.

4 **Go right** at the fork by the metal gate. Pass a waymarked Wealden Walks post. Further on, cross a plank bridge and walk along between two hedges. **Head right** up the hill at the T-junction with a driveway and waymarked post on the left. Halfway up the hill, leave the stony track to walk **straight ahead** past a waymarked post on the bridleway. GPS can be patchy in these woods. Follow this sometimes muddy but obvious bridleway through this archetypal mixed woodland. Keep walking along the track through a coppiced area. **Walk right** past the low marker post and on up the hill when you reach a track. Climb a little way.

5 **Easy to miss**: **go left**, leaving the track by the very short waymarker post. **Turn left** down the hill along the tarmac bridleway. Reach a hedged driveway and timber-framed house. **Turn left** in front of the timber-framed house at the waymarked Wealden Walks post: this house was probably once the home of a hammersmith. Cross the stone bridge over the stream and along the bridleway to the **right**. At the signpost, **continue** on the bridleway. It runs along the fence. The bridleway joins a tarmac track. Pass a red tile-hung house and walk **straight on** along the unsigned bridleway in front of some garages. This is Hare Holt. Walk along the top of the field and through a gate. Walk along a wooded track and go through a waymarked wooden walk-through fence.

6 **Turn left** along the footpath and track. It's an easy walking surface but up a hill. Cross the stile or go through a gate and continue climbing until the top of the hill where the path curves towards the house. Go **diagonally right**, leaving the track, to follow the footpath along the hedgerow at the waymarked post.

7 By another waymarked post, climb over a stile beside a gate and walk **straight on**. Pass a Batt's Wood noticeboard and walk **straight on** past the noticeboard and, almost immediately, **walk left** at a second marker post. **Follow the curving track** as it gently descends to a marker post by a fence at the back of the house where you **walk right** along the track. Pass another Batt's Wood noticeboard and marker post. Walk along a fence.

8 Go through a gate and **turn left** to follow a footpath through Wadhurst Park estate. See a lake to your distant right. Pass a signpost and walk **straight on**, and past another signpost and down a slope. Walk between some trees, over a stream/ditch and past another signpost to walk along the edge of the trees on the mud track. Then walk **straight** past another signpost and, after a few more steps, at the next signpost, near a wire fence, **walk right** across the stream, through a tall kissing gate and start walking up the hill.

9 **Turn left** at the small signpost to walk along the grassy footpath. Go through the gate and walk **straight ahead** along the fence. Climb over a stile and walk **straight on** through the grassy field on the footpath. Climb over a stile.

10 **Turn left** at the signpost. Cross a bridge and immediately **turn right** along the footpath at the post. Pass a marker post and cross a footbridge with a signpost just after it. Walk **right** along the footpath towards a gate, passing a low marker post by a tree stump and footbridge. Climb over the stile beside the gate. Walk straight up the hill and **bear left** across a waymarked bridge. Walk on alongside the fence and climb over the stile.

11 **Turn left** at the four-way signpost on the bridge to walk along the tree-lined footpath. Cross a bridge. Walk a few steps past a wire fence and **turn right** to walk through an idyllic glade. **Turn left** at a corner with two stiles and walk up through the woods. Look for the path up through the trees. Once you've taken a few steps, it becomes more obvious. Follow it up through the woods and, eventually, along a wire fence. This is a long horrible hill to climb on a muddy path but the woods are serene. Go through a gate and leave Combe Wood. Walk **straight ahead** between the trees. **Turn right** at the signpost to walk through a copse.

12 Cross the stile by the post and walk **diagonally left** along the footpath. Walk along the fence and pass an old stile to continue on along the wire fence. Enjoy the views and walk all the way to the end of this field. Cross a waymarked stile and **walk right** along the fenced track.

13 At the three-way signpost, **turn right** along a bridleway through Sharnden Old Manor Farm. Walk up the fenced track. Walk **straight ahead** at the signpost by a house.

14 At the end, **turn left** and climb over the first stile to walk down through a sheep field. Where the concrete track ends, walk on towards a footbridge. **Cross** and **turn right** to walk along the stream. After a while, the path curves left: it's not obvious but climbs up to a four-way signpost. **Turn right** at this crossroads and walk on. At the fork where there's a yellow waymarker emblem attached to a tree, **walk right**. Go through a waymarked gate and continue on, looking out for old stones. Go through a broken (!) metal gate. Cross a footbridge and walk along a stream. Walk **straight on** along the grassy path. Emerge at a cottage.

15 At the white signpost, **turn left** to Mayfield along the road. Pass some typical High Weald timber-boarded houses and walk up the hill. This road returns to Mayfield but we are going to explore Vicarage Wood, the site of a second foundry. **Turn right** at the signed footpath just after where *SLOW* is painted on the road. Pass a marker post and walk up the hill. Pass Coggins Mill and walk **straight ahead** at another waymarked post past some houses.

16 Go through a kissing gate and walk along the footpath into the woods. Cross a small footbridge and walk up some steps. Walk **diagonally right** at a Wealden Walks marker post. The path is unclear so use map and directions **carefully**. After 50m, **turn right** at the next marker post and walk down the slope to pass another marker post. Walk on across the long, narrow footbridge. At the three-way signpost, near a stile, walk **slightly left** staying in the woods. **Keep left** and walk along the banks of this wide stream with small rocks and running water. At a clearing, continue along the mud track, to walk roughly parallel to the stream which you can hear but not see.

17 **Walk left** at a waymarked post across a wooden bridge on what was once the route of the Mayfield to Tunbridge Wells coach road, but don't miss the Mayfield Foundry noticeboard, diagonally opposite the post before you cross the wooden bridge. **Ignore** the offshoot path to the left. Walk up towards a metal gate and, just before you reach it, **turn left** at the three-way marker post to walk on through the woods. Cross a flat stone bridge over the narrowing stream and be careful of the protruding bricks on the next stretch of path.

18 Emerge from the trees: if you look back you should see a yellow waymarker arrow stuck to a narrow trunk. Walk **straight up** the hill and along the trees. Pass a stile beside an oast house and walk on along a mud track beside the fence. Go through a kissing gate amid a line of trees. Walk a few steps and walk through a gap beside a stile then pass a Wealden Walks marker post. Walk on along a fence.

19 At the four-way signpost, **turn right** along a footpath. Climb over a stile beside a metal gate and continue **straight ahead** along the top edge of a field. Climb over one final stile and cross a mud track. Walk past the marker post and up the steps. Head across a football field to join a concrete footpath through the park. Walk up towards some buildings. At the road, **turn left** and pass the entrance to Mayfield School. When you reach the High Street, **turn right** and then **left** down Holders Lane to return to the car park.

WEALDEN WOODS & THE RIVER MEDWAY

DISTANCE: 14.8KM/9.2MILES » **TOTAL ASCENT:** 235M/771FT » **START GR:** TQ 531373 » **TIME:** ALLOW 3.5-4 HOURS PLUS STOPS » **SATNAV:** TN3 9QX » **MAP:** OS EXPLORER 135, ASHDOWN FOREST, 1:25,000 » **REFRESHMENTS:** DORSET ARMS, WITHYHAM (18TH-CENTURY ALEHOUSE AND GARDEN); THE JUNCTION INN, AND BAKERY AND SHOP BY START IN GROOMBRIDGE » **NAVIGATION:** STRAIGHTFORWARD. CAREFUL NEAR THE LAKE IN JOCKEY'S WOOD.

MOTTSMILL STREAM

09 Wealden Woods & the River Medway

14.8km/9.2miles

A straightforward but off the beaten track idyllic loop which passes through two rare ecological habitats.

Groombridge » Rocks Wood » High Weald Landscape Trail » Buckhurst Park » Withyham » River Medway » Forest Way » Groombridge

Start
Groombridge Memorial Hall car park, Station Road. Roadside, if full.
GR: TQ 531373.

The Walk
Our route begins in the village of Groombridge, on the border between Kent and East Sussex, and heads south on the High Weald Landscape Trail. Make your way through crop fields to some Arcadian grazing pastures. Could this be an ancient 'den' or woodland pasture used for pannage? This was the practice of feeding pigs on acorns and fallen nuts in an autumnal forest. Early farmers drove their pigs for seasonal fattening and, as they did so, they helped form the unique radiating pattern of ancient routeways which characterises this High Weald landscape.

Follow Mottsmill Stream into a rather special gill woodland. Rocks Wood includes Penns Rocks, a Site of Special Scientific Interest. This steep-sided wooded valley leaves outcrops of Cretaceous rock exposed. The Ardingly sandstone is formed of the Hastings bed and the resulting 'sandrock' is a nationally rare habitat. The warm, moist microclimate supports a rich community of ferns, mosses and liverworts. Further on, Legg Wood is notable too for its springs which rise where sandy soils meet the sticky clay. A climb towards Coppice Wood allows some far-reaching views, descending through the historic parkland of Buckhurst Park estate. Previous owners included the earls and dukes of Dorset, hence the name of the pub at Withyham. This 18th-century alehouse with garden may provide a good place to refuel.

We cross Forest Way (optional shortcut) and follow Wealdway on a scenic and oh-so-peaceful footpath by the River Medway through a conservation area. Paths may be overgrown with nettles so shorts aren't recommended. This Medway floodplain can be damp underfoot. Butterflies, moths and damselflies skitter. Approach the river quietly and listen carefully: the water is a magnet for wildlife and you never know what you might see. When leaving the floodplain, look out for the rare black poplar trees planted by Sussex Wildlife Trust. The habitats explored on this walk deserve our protection.

09 WEALDEN WOODS & THE RIVER MEDWAY

Directions – Wealden Woods & the River Medway

❺ Cross Station Road to walk up Corseley Road. At the top, walk **straight ahead** past Orchard Rise and a marker post. Pass the school and walk **straight ahead** past another marker post, staying on the road. **Curve left** on Corseley Road passing the High Weald Landscape Trail (HWLT) post. Walk down the hill. Pass Forest Way and the waterworks.

2 **Turn right** across a waymarked stile to follow Sussex Border Path (SBP). Cross a footbridge and another stile and pass beneath bridge 567; it is from here that the walk takes off! At the signposted junction, walk **diagonally left** along the footpath through the crop field. Cross two stiles and follow the HWLT through this grazing field. Go through an SBP marked gate. At the fork, **veer left** (on SBP and HWLT) through the woods. Walk **straight ahead** at the next marker post (still following SBP and HWLT) and pass the gate, following the signpost **straight ahead** along the lane. Pass Valley Cottage and climb the steep hill on this easy surface.

3 **Turn left** across the stile, following the SBP. Descend and cross the waymarked footbridge. **Turn right** along the footpath through grazing pastures. Walk along the stream and **turn right** across another footbridge. Walk on along the footpath through the woodland. Pass a marker post and cross a drive. **Be careful**, the first marker points ahead but almost immediately **turn left** at the **second, easy-to-miss**, marker stump. Cross the footbridge and then a stile, following the waymarked footpath up the field and through the gate at the top. Cross the stile and follow the signed footpath **straight ahead**. Climb the short slope, cross a stile and follow the HWLT onwards past the rocks.

Pass through the route which is marked *Walkers' Gap* beside the gate and follow the HWLT **diagonally right** along the trees. Go through the gap. Immediately **turn right** through a metal gate followed by the HWLT and walk on. Note the waymarker emblems on the post and walk on through the brick gateposts. Note another HWLT marker on lone gatepost and follow drive **right** passing another emblem on a wall of Home Place. **Walk on** along the drive and HWLT until you reach the road.

4 Cross the road (careful!). **Walk left** and soon, at the waymarked sign, **turn right** through the walkers' gap stile following the HWLT. Go through the gate and walk **straight on** down the hill. Pass a marker post and follow a track between two fences. Go through the walkers' gap stile and walk on along the fence. Cross a stile and follow the HWLT through Legg Wood. Cross another stile and **turn right** across a footbridge. Climb another stile and walk **straight ahead** across the grazing pasture. Cross another stile.

5 **Turn right** along Whitehouse Lane. At the T-junction, **carefully** cross the road and follow the HWLT **straight ahead** into the woods along this ancient cobbled path. At the marker post, **turn left** across the footbridge and stile to follow the waymarked footpath **right**. Climb to the summit, enjoying fab views. Cross a stile and continue **straight ahead** along the footpath across the hilltop, strewn with wild flowers in season. **Ignore** the stile and walk **straight ahead** following the signed HWLT down and a slight **diagonal left** to the stile in the trees. Cross and **walk left** along this old cobbled trail between the fences. Pass a marker post and walk **straight ahead**. **Walk right** at the next marker post along the tarmac driveway of Buckhurst Park. Pass The Old Mill House and Saunders, cross a bridge over a stream and pass a cricket ground.

ENJOY VIEWS ACROSS THE HIGH WEALD

Directions – Wealden Woods & the River Medway continued...

6 At the road, see the Dorset Arms. Cross and **turn left**, following the HWLT. Walk along the pavement, passing Withyham village hall and car park and a house. Walk along Withyham Road on the verge around the bend and across Hewkins Bridge. **Turn right** across the stile. Walk **straight across** the field following Wealdway (WW). Cross a stile and continue. Cross a stile.

7 This is Forest Way.* Walk **straight across** the track and over another stile to follow WW along the River Medway. Enter the conservation area (dogs on leads). Pass a pond and walk to a stile in the corner. Cross a stile and follow WW along the footpath. At the signpost, keep walking **straight ahead** on the narrow path. Go up some steps and **turn right** following a waymarker signpost. Walk along the edge of the field. At the lane, walk **right** through the gate and **straight on** along WW on the tarmac drive. Some way along, pass a marker post. At the end, **turn left** to walk through the houses, keeping dogs on leads.

> *Turn right** for a shortcut back to Groombridge. Rejoin the main route in Point 9 to return to the start.

8 Cross the road, and the stile, to follow WW **straight ahead**. Pass a couple of marker posts and walk on, following the track up the river. Just where the river curves left and the path seems to disappear, a footbridge appears. **Walk left** across the footbridge and then **turn right** following WW past the marker post. Continue on along the course of the river. Cross a waymarked bridge and soon emerge in a field. Walk **straight on** along the edge. Pass a marker post and cross a waymarked footbridge. Walk **straight ahead** on WW, along the side of the stream. Follow WW right and walk away, leaving the footbridge directly behind you, to take a path through the crops. Cross a concrete bridge across the river and walk **straight ahead** on the SBP. Walk past Ham Farm, along a hedged path and then driveway.

9 **Cross with care**. **Turn right** and walk along the verge for a short distance. After the curve, **turn left** (shortcut rejoins here) to walk 2km along Forest Way Country Park. Cross the road to walk the final section which leads you back to the waterworks at Groombridge. Retrace your steps to Station Road.

A CIRCUIT FROM THE SOUTH CHASE OF THE ASHDOWN FOREST

DISTANCE: 16.6KM/10.3MILES » **TOTAL ASCENT**: 416M/1,364FT » **START GR**: TQ 466271 » **TIME**: ALLOW 4.5 HOURS PLUS STOPS » **SATNAV**: TN22 3BJ » **MAP**: OS EXPLORER 135, ASHDOWN FOREST, 1:25,000 » **REFRESHMENTS**: BARNSGATE MANOR RESTAURANT AND TEA ROOM; THE HURSTWOOD, HIGH HURSTWOOD; OCCASIONAL CAFE, OAST FARM, BUXTED; THE PIG & BUTCHER, FIVE ASH DOWN; THE FORESTERS ARMS, FAIRWARP » **NAVIGATION**: LOOK OUT FOR WEALDWAY MARKER POSTS TO HELP YOU, PARTICULARLY THROUGH ASHDOWN FOREST WHERE NAVIGATION CAN BE TRICKY. NOTE, MARKER POSTS MAY NOT ALWAYS HAVE WEALDWAY EMBLEMS. USE DIRECTIONS CAREFULLY IN UNSIGNED SECTION OF POINT 8.

A WOODLAND PATH

10 A Circuit from the South Chase of the Ashdown Forest

16.6km/10.3miles

This intricate and challenging loop explores the south chase of the Ashdown Forest and uses surrounding rural tracks to circle past several good refreshment stops and fine views.

Ashdown Forest » Wealdway » Barnsgate Manor » Quarry Wood » High Hurstwood » Stonehouse » Wealdway » Five Ash Down » Hendall Wood » Wealdway » Brickfield Meadow Nature Reserve » Fairwarp » Ashdown Forest

Start

Shepherds car park, on the B2026, north of Fairwarp church. GR: TQ 466271.

The Walk

Our circular trail begins in the south chase and uses sections of Wealdway, a long-distance route. Navigation through the forest can be tricky and some paths may be muddy, but these woodlands and heaths are something special. This route ventures into lesser-known pockets and there may not be another soul to be seen. Woodlands vary from a patch of dark 'fairy tale' forest, mysterious and mossy, to Scots pine reaching up majestically from a gill, to mixed woodland strewn with rocks, bluebells and leaf litter. Happen upon a heath or enjoy a view from a ridge. A stream babbles along a gully, foxes share their paths and deer may pause to study you, but civilisation is never far away and this walk offers plenty of refreshment stops. The terrace at Barnsgate Manor tea rooms has uplifting views, there's a part-time cafe at Oast Farm and The Foresters Arms is a welcoming walkers' pub, well-placed for a hearty home-cooked lunch near the end of your walk.

The path through Quarry Wood gives a good sense of an ancient iron ore track and would have been widened by the passage of frequent horse-drawn carts. Valuable Wealden clay was dug up in the search for iron ore and both needed transporting: iron ore to a furnace and clay to a brickworks. Sunken Perrymans Lane was one such route to Fairwarp. Towards the end of our trail, as we approach Fairwarp, we walk through Furnace Wood, its name a clue to the importance of the iron industry in this area. At its height, many High Weald inhabitants would have been somehow involved, perhaps employed in digging ore, cutting wood or transporting raw materials and products.

Look out for 'red' streams, indicative of iron-rich soil. Beside one such brook, Sussex Wildlife Trust has a traditionally managed meadow reserve (seasonal grazing – dogs on leads). Brickfield Meadow is a welcome food source for invertebrates; the nectar of plants such as pignut provides food for moths like the chimney sweeper. On a summer's day, listen out for Roesel's bush-cricket and count the wild flowers.

10 A CIRCUIT FROM THE SOUTH CHASE OF THE ASHDOWN FOREST

Directions – A Circuit from the South Chase of the Ashdown Forest

⊙➤ Walk past the wooden posts which form a vehicle barrier and along a grassy (open access) forest path. Pass a house. **Turn left** at the crossroads to join a wide grassy path. Walk through the forest. Glimpse occasional houses through trees on both sides and reach a clearing. The path descends. Shortly after the footbridge, look for a four-way wooden signpost.

2 **Turn left** along Wealdway (WW), marked in yellow. This narrow path can have muddy stretches. Pass a WW marker stump and heathland opens up to your right. **Walk right** at an easy-to-miss marker stump where WW diverts down an inauspicious path. **Walk up this** narrow track through the heath. At the wide grassy path, **turn left** staying on the unsigned WW. The path becomes more wooded.

Turn right at the WW marker stump to follow WW. Head through the trees then cross a driveway and descend. **Turn left** along the tarmac driveway. Pass May Cottage on the left and then another house on your right. Pass Brown's Brook Cottage and walk **straight ahead** past the WW yellow marker post. Cross a footbridge. Climb this mud track as it wends through dense woodland. Soon, the canopy lightens.

Turn right at the large WW sign, following the narrow path up a steep slope. Pass a house on your left and a faded WW marker stump. Walk along the side of a clearing. At the top of the hill there's a large WW sign; **turn right** along the stony path. Pass two WW marker stumps. Keep **straight ahead** on the footpath. See a distant house to your right. Follow the tarmac and stony path as it veers left and snakes onwards.

3 **Turn right** at the three-way marker post, leaving the metalled path to follow the signed bridleway. Head for a gate and go through to walk **straight ahead**. Walk through Barnsgate Manor where there are some wonderful views (and a nice cup of tea!) to be enjoyed. Before the toilet block, **turn left**, following *Way Out* signs and walk along the driveway.

4 Follow the signed footpath **straight across** the road and past Stroods Lodge. Go through the kissing gate and walk **straight ahead** on the concrete path. Pass a house and then a pond.

5 **Turn right** joining Vanguard Way before the cattle grid. Go through the small gate and follow Vanguard Way between the hedges. At the wooden waymarker sign, stay on this hedged track which curves left. Cross the stile and walk on through Quarry Wood. Feel the old iron ore track beneath your feet. At the crossroads with a small signpost, follow the footpath **straight ahead**. At the waymarker, keep **straight ahead** on this ancient track.

6 **Turn left*** at the road and, a short distance along, **turn left** through the kissing gate following the footpath, as signed, down the slope. Go through another kissing gate and continue **straight ahead** on the footpath. Descend across the field and, beyond the oak, go through another kissing gate. Cross a footbridge over a stream. Glimpse a red-brick building. Follow the path. Go through a gate and cross the road.

> ⟳ *Or, if you need a shortcut to Fairwarp, now's your chance, but **we don't recommend this**: the road is narrow with high hedges and blind corners. **Turn right** along Perrymans Lane. Pass Perrymans Farm. At the end **turn right** on to the A26 then **immediately left** down steep Oldlands Hill. Pass Oldlands Farm and use the footbridge by the ford. At Oldlands Hall, **turn left** to walk along the lane to Fairwarp and rejoin the main route at Point 13.

7 At the road, look for the signpost slightly to the right. Cross and rejoin Vanguard Way and walk **straight ahead** up the signed footpath towards Holy Trinity church but, before you draw level with the church, **turn right** through a kissing gate to follow Vanguard Way. Pass above a tennis court and through a kissing gate to follow the signed Vanguard Way ahead. After a while, go through another gate and onwards to another gate. **Turn left** following Vanguard Way along the road and up the hill a short way. Follow unsigned Vanguard Way **right** along a mud track. The path becomes concrete. Pass Royal Oak Farm and some houses. At the T-junction, **turn right** and follow the lane down past the playing fields and to the pub, The Hurstwood.

Directions – A Circuit from the South Chase of the Ashdown Forest continued...

8 **Turn right** along the road and soon **turn left** down Perrymans Lane. Cross the bridge. **Turn left** following the wooden-waymarked footpath past several houses and along a sometimes-muddy path for a while. **Turn right** before the gate to go up the steps following the official path diversion and walk along the fence heading in the same direction as before. Go over another stile and walk **straight ahead** to follow the narrow footpath. Follow the path down some steps. **Walk left** through a wide metal gate. **Turn right** to follow the footpath marker post. At Rocks Lane, **turn right** and walk along the lane.

9 At the A26, **walk left** and then almost **immediately turn left** over the cattle grid along the signed footpath. This hedged tarmac track is peaceful. Pass farm buildings and, at the end of the track, climb over the waymarked stile. Walk **diagonally right** along the unsigned footpath towards **two gates** in the bottom corner of the field by the trees. Go through the open gateway on the **left**. Walk down the next grazing field and along the fence to a waymarked footbridge in the corner. Cross and follow the footpath straight up the hill through the cow field towards an electricity post. Beside the post, see a metal fence panel with a footplate to help you climb over. On the other side, **turn left** along the grassy track on the left-hand side of the hedge. At the end of the hedge, some steps lead down. **Turn right** along the lane. Pass some houses, including an interesting almshouse, and a school car park.

10 **Turn right** along WW to walk down the hill on the tarmac footpath beside the grass verge of the A272. Pass Noah's Ark. Look out for an *Oast Farm Buxted* sign and **turn right** along the road towards the farm. At the gate to the farm, fishing lake and cafe, take the narrow path to the **left** of the pedestrian gate. Walk along a footpath, then cross a stile and walk along this clear but narrow track (nettles!). Go through a metal gate and walk **straight ahead** along the garage driveway. Proceed across the grass to the small traffic island of the main junction. Look across at the road sign and see the wooden waymarker to its right. Cross the road.

11 Follow WW into the woods. Pass a marker post and stand at the edge of Cobdown Lane and look across to the other side: at about two o'clock to your right, there's a rather insignificant gap which is your footpath. Continue along the footpath, going in the same direction through the woods. You may spot a rather submerged WW marker stump. Pass a permissive footpath marker stump. Follow the fence past a house. See a WW arrow on a fence post and walk **straight on** through grassland. Pass a marker post and walk **straight ahead** following the footpath to the left through Hendall Wood. Descend a slope and cross a footbridge over a stream.

Walk **straight ahead** between the fences. Go through a gate and follow WW **diagonally left** between the fences, and on up the slope. **Turn left** through the gate, past the farm buildings and dog kennel entrance and follow the signed WW up the rough lane. At the top, see a WW emblem on the gatepost. Walk on a few metres to the four-way marker post.

12 **Turn left** following WW along the track and enjoy the view. At the next junction stay on the track as it curves right and go through the black automatic gate. Pass through another gate and follow the signed WW ahead. Follow the track **left** around the house. Pass through a kissing gate and **turn left** to keep going on the same direction along WW, as signed. Go through a kissing gate and walk on through a rather dark but atmospheric woodland. (**Careful**: rocky path, steep drops and steps!) **Turn right** at the signpost, along WW. Pass a marker post and descend some steep steps. Cross a footbridge over a ditch and walk on **straight ahead**, following the WW marker post. Follow the path left across a footbridge over a stream. **Turn right** through the gate to enjoy Sussex Wildlife Trust's nature reserve, Brickfield Meadow. Walk through the far gate and **turn right**, passing a WW marker post.

13 **Turn left** along the road. (Shortcut rejoins here.) There's a slight incline but you'll soon reach The Foresters Arms at Fairwarp. After the pub, **turn right** along the residential lane and unsigned footpath. **Keep left** at the fork with the stone footpath marker. Pass Sunmore and the drive to New Stone Cottage but, after a few steps, leave the track to **turn left** along an unsigned narrow mud footpath. At a fork, take a step or two to the **right** and then **turn left** up the slope. Reach a wide path or ride and **turn left**: you are back on the path near the start. **Turn right** to retrace your footsteps to Shepherds car park.

SECTION 3

Orchard Country

The High Weald is particularly suited to growing apples and several of our trails include orchard paths. In season, the fruit ripens to red and marks the passing of another year; walking can be a marvellous way to connect with local food sources and the rhythms of life. Views here may take on a semblance of the pastoral idyll as cows and sheep graze in the fields and boundaries criss-cross over rolling hills to shaws and oast houses. On old tithe maps hop gardens abound, but, nowadays, the distinctive oast buildings tend to be private residences. Railways and forgotten industries speak of a prosperous past but life hasn't always been easy; many tracks are ancient routes, pressed down through the centuries by creaking cartwheels or determined footfall, and used to transport goods, legal or otherwise. Stories of smugglers' exploits echo but the Battle of Goudhurst embodies notable drama. Enjoy.

KIPLING'S HIGH WEALD: POOK'S HILL & RIDGE VIEWS

DISTANCE: 10.5KM/6.5MILES » **TOTAL ASCENT**: 209M/685FT » **START GR**: TQ 673246 » **TIME**: ALLOW 2.5–3 HOURS PLUS STOPS » **SATNAV**: TN19 7ET » **MAP**: OS EXPLORERS 124, HASTINGS & BEXHILL, AND 136, HIGH WEALD, BOTH 1:25,000 **REFRESHMENTS**: THE BEAR INN, THE ROSE AND CROWN, BURWASH; THE WHEEL INN, BURWASH WEALD; NATIONAL TRUST MULBERRY TEA ROOM AT BATEMAN'S » **NAVIGATION**: STRAIGHTFORWARD.

A FARMER WORKING IN A HAY FIELD

11 Kipling's High Weald: Pook's Hill & Ridge Views

10.5km/6.5miles

A straightforward loop through Rudyard Kipling country with some fine views.

Burwash » Holton Hill » Lower Bough » Burwash Weald » Bateman's » Burwash

Start

The Square (free) car park, Burwash. GR: TQ 673246.

The Walk

This is a relaxing, shortish walk which enables you to explore the heart of the High Weald. The walk begins on Burwash High Street where 15th and 16th-century houses lurk behind the Georgian facades of many buildings. Back in 1252, King Henry III recognised the village's importance as a trading centre and authorised a weekly market and a summer fair.

This route descends north into the Weald on an easy track, before climbing back up on the approach to Burwash Weald – but the resulting views from the ridge are worth the effort. Burwash is best known for its association with Rudyard Kipling. The author lived at Bateman's (now a National Trust property), in what is thought to be an old ironmaster's house. From Burwash Weald, descend to where this house sits beside a stream and mill.

Kipling's body of work may now evoke controversy but he was undeniably a prolific and world-renowned writer. In *Puck of Pook's Hill*, he creates a magical being or ancient fairy, Puck, with a penchant for storytelling who entertains two children by weaving tales about the past. Although it may seem deceptively simple, an exploration of the elements of landscape, the disjointed nature of time and how we make sense of the past through storytelling are wrapped up in the guise of this children's story. As you pass near Point 9, it's just possible that you are walking in the landscape that inspired *Pook's Hill*.

'A Three-Part Song', a poem within *Puck of Pook's Hill*, tells of the three main landscapes of Sussex: the Weald, Romney Marsh and the South Downs. The second verse is about the Weald:

I've buried my heart in a ferny hill,
Twix' a liddle low shaw an' a great high gill.
Oh, hop-bine yaller an' woodsmoke blue,
I reckon you'll keep her middling true!

The walk passes near restored Park Mill and the main entrance to Bateman's, and you may wish to explore the atmospheric house and gardens.

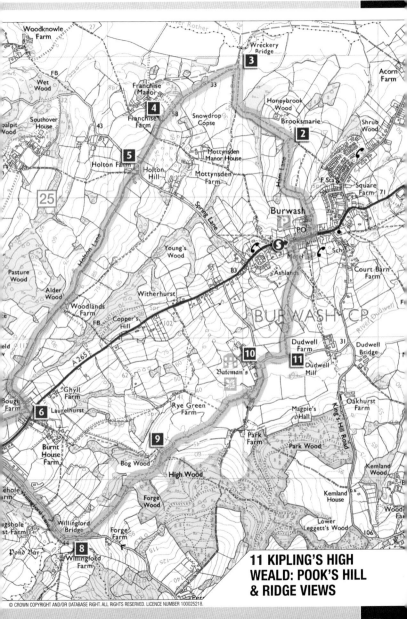

11 KIPLING'S HIGH WEALD: POOK'S HILL & RIDGE VIEWS

Directions – Kipling's High Weald: Pook's Hill & Ridge Views

➎ Exit the car park and **turn right**. Cross and walk along the High Street. **Turn left** at The Rose and Crown sign along the public footpath (Ham Lane). Pass the pub and continue **straight ahead** along the half-made track. It curves and descends.

2 **Turn left** through a kissing gate with a yellow waymarker signing the footpath **slightly diagonally right** across the field. Go through a small waymarked gate in the corner of the field. Continue **straight ahead** on the footpath through the wood. Follow the footpath **left** at the marker post. Cross a waymarked footbridge and go through a gate. **Turn right** and cross the footbridge. Then, cross another footbridge and walk **straight on** along the edge of the grazing field.

3 **Turn left** across the stile and follow the footpath up the edge of the field. Go through a gate and join a bridleway to walk **straight ahead** through the grazing fields. At the top of the hill, walk **straight ahead** through a gate in the left-hand corner. Walk up along the footpath until you see a stile in the fence on your **right**. Climb over.

4 **Turn left** along the bridleway and lane, climbing steadily in the same direction as before. Pass a signpost and an orchard to your left and enjoy views to the right. Pass a house and go through a distinctive gate with a cartwheel.

5 **Turn left** along the lane for a few steps, passing the farm. **Turn right** at the signpost and follow the bridleway to the left of a gate signed *Holton Farmhouse*. Stay on the bridleway. This very easy path runs alongside grazing fields and through Wealden copses and gills. Continue **straight ahead** past a signpost, climbing steadily on the bridleway until the way ahead is barred by a padlocked gate. **Turn left** along the bridleway at the signpost with a *Paths to Prosperity* sign. Follow the bridleway as it curves past a couple of houses to the main road.

6 **Do not** cross the road but **double back on yourself** following the footpath sign. Walk **right** up the hill. Go **straight ahead**, leaving the track to climb over a stile. Follow the fenced footpath through livery fields. Climb over another stile and walk **straight ahead**. Pass a house and continue **straight on** and through a gap in a hedge. You are walking along a ridge and appealing vistas open up over the Burwash Weald. Look out

for nesting birds and pheasants. Pass an oast house and follow the narrow footpath past the marker post. Go through a waymarked gate and walk past The Bough to follow the footpath to the road.

7 **Turn left** and walk along the pavement beside the main road. **Turn right** down the lane opposite The Wheel Inn (Harvey's, beer garden). Pass various houses and then the oast house and then Mill Lands. The lane becomes more sunken with high hedges: **care needed!** Pass a signpost but stay on the road. Descend further. Cross a bridge over a pond.

8 **Turn left** at the signpost and follow the footpath across the stile. Once over, **turn right** and walk up edge of the field. Climb over another stile and walk **straight on** along the footpath. Follow the top edge of the field and go through a gap and then into a copse. Cross a couple of stiles. Follow the waymarked footpath **diagonally right**. Go through a kissing gate and walk **diagonally right** on the waymarked footpath.

9 **Walk straight on** at the marker post following the waymarked footpath. At the signposts, walk **straight ahead** but follow the landowner's directions to pass through the gate on the left enabling you to walk separately from the cows. **Turn left** at the marker post through a gate and then straight on. Go through a kissing gate and continue onwards. **Walk straight on** at the signpost. Notice the National Trust arrows: you are now near Bateman's. Walk over a dam or sluice gate. Walk on following the path. Pass between the pond and the mill house. At the signpost, **turn left** along the waymarked bridleway. Pass the oast house. See Bateman's on the left.

10 **Turn right** away from the house at the T-junction and waymarker signpost. (If you wish to visit the house, divert a few metres left to the main entrance.)

11 **Turn left** at the signpost. Climb over the stile and walk up the field. Pass a signpost and head **slightly diagonally right**. Walk through a waymarked gate and along the cordoned-off side of a grazing field. Pass through a second gate and walk **straight on**. Go through another gate and across a footbridge. Follow the signed footpath **left** up the hill. Pass the pub garden and arrive back at the car park.

ANCIENT ROUTEWAYS: BENENDEN TO ROLVENDEN

DISTANCE: 12.1KM/7.5MILES » **TOTAL ASCENT**: 212M/696FT » **START GR**: TQ 810328 » **TIME**: 3 HOURS PLUS STOPS
SATNAV: TN17 4DE » **MAP**: OS EXPLORER 125, ROMNEY MARSH, RYE & WINCHELSEA » **REFRESHMENTS**: THE BULL AT
BENENDEN, COMMUNITY SHOP AND CAFE AT BENENDEN; THE BULL INN, ROLVENDEN; THE WOODCOCK INN, IDEN GREEN; HOLE
PARK GARDENS TEA ROOMS OPEN SELECTED DAYS » **NAVIGATION**: STRAIGHTFORWARD.

AN OAST HOUSE

12 Ancient Routeways: Benenden to Rolvenden

12.1km/7.5miles

A tranquil route from Benenden to Rolvenden through ancient woodland and agricultural pastures returning on the High Weald Landscape Trail through orchards and sheep country.

Benenden » Nine Acre Wood » Stepneyford Bridge » Hole Park » Rolvenden » High Weald Landscape Trail » Willerd's Hill Wood » Strawberry Wood » Benenden

Start

Benenden Village Hall car park.
GR: TQ 810328. Or roadside parking by the village green.

The Walk

This lovely walk is shortish but there's lots to see and it makes for a good outing. Our trail begins in Benenden beside a pretty village green backed by an imposing church. The Domesday Book suggests that 'Benindene' was one of only four places in the Weald to have a church. Look out for the Gibbon Building, opened as a free school in 1609 and still in use today as a school building.

There's a sense of movement in this landscape and it's not just your feet walking but time passing. Feel the ancient woodland tracks beneath your boots and know that others have trodden your path. A typical droveway may be narrow, deeply sunken and edged with trees, its impressive banks brightened by wild flowers. The Wealden iron industry boomed in this area, building on the industry of the Romans. Look out for remnants of the hammer and furnace ponds, and in Strawberry Wood you can see a restored culvert which may have been built by the iron masters. This stone bridge enables water to flow through a tunnel beneath the path. It was certainly designed for industrial use but nobody's sure quite when it was built. Nearby Dingleden was the site of fulling mills, in which wooden hammers beat the cloths to produce a dense felted product, and the culvert is as likely to have been used to help transport cloth as iron.

Hole Park Gardens is open on selected days, with home-made teas and light lunches served in the Coach House. In Rolvenden, you can't miss imposing St Mary the Virgin church, largely unchanged since 1480. Take a look at the Squire's pew and its Chippendale chairs which offer a view down onto the congregation. It was built for the Gibbons family of Hole Park and isn't it interesting how when you walk the interconnections between people, history and communities reveal themselves in all their many layers?

Directions – Ancient Routeways: Benenden to Rolvenden

↪ Turn **left** out of the car park and **right** down the lane opposite The Bull Inn, passing the war memorial. Walk along Walkhurst Road passing an interesting mix of historic and modern housing. Follow the lane as it curves left, **ignoring** the first waymarker beside a metal gate where there are some old outbuildings. Walk down the hill and pass a driveway.

2 At the signpost, **turn right** along this idyllic footpath beside a tree-lined stream. Watch out for an interesting stone section – this path is well cared for! Walk on along what must surely be an ancient Wealden track.

3 Before a metal gate, **walk right**, following a yellow arrow on a tree and stay on the track as it curves. Are these ancient iron workings to the right? Glimpse orchards through the trees. Pass a gate and continue **straight ahead** along a hedged track. Stay on the grassy hedged track when you pass a kissing gate. This track is lined by wild flowers in summer. The track curves. Pass a timber-framed oast house. The track becomes tarmac and you walk past several residences. **Ignore** a couple of footpath signposts leading left then right and **stay on this tarmac track**. This quiet hedged lane (byway) undulates and has the boundary banks of a droveway.

4 **Turn right** along the lane at the junction, following the signed NCR 18 for approx. 1.5km. Occasional cars! This tree-lined quiet lane undulates and then there's a long, steady climb. Pass a kissing gate and signposts on the right and left. **Continue** past a postbox on the left and Green Lane Farmhouse.

5 **Turn left** at the signposted footpath. Go through a kissing gate and a gap in the hedge to your **left**, spotting a waymarker arrow. **Turn right** to follow the footpath with a hedge on your right and an orchard on your left. Continue **straight ahead** to another waymarker arrow and walk past the post, continuing **straight ahead**. Pass a fenced plantation area. Cross a tarmac drive and at the path junction **keep left** along the grassy path, continuing in roughly the same direction along the laurel hedge. At the end, walk **straight on** through a timberyard and **turn left** through the wide gap towards a big house. Hole Park Gardens are open on selected days when the Coach House cafe is open too. **Walk right** on the waymarked footpath. Just before the entrance, go through a small gate. Walk **diagonally left** through a grazing field towards large conifer trees to a kissing gate on the far edge.

12 ANCIENT ROUTEWAYS: BENENDEN TO ROLVENDEN

Directions – Ancient Routeways: Benenden to Rolvenden continued...

6   Walk **diagonally left** and over a plank between two fishing ponds. Go through a kissing gate and walk **diagonally left**. Climb on up the slope passing a war memorial on the far side of the field. Pass a marker on the fence. Walk **diagonally left** and pass a marooned stile and marker post. Follow the footpath towards the windmill. Walk past the mill and the house to a kissing gate.

7   **Turn left** along the main road and walk along the path into Rolvenden, passing The Bull Inn. **Turn right** along Rolvenden High Street. Pass the general stores and The Star pub. Stay on the High Street where it bends at the junction.

8   **Turn right** along the signed High Weald Landscape Trail (HWLT) beside Rolvenden Primary School and opposite the church. Go through a kissing gate and follow the white HWLT **diagonally left**. About halfway along the opposite edge of the school playing fields, walk past a marker post on the public footpath through a copse and **head left**. **Turn left** along the footpath at the crop field. Walk **diagonally right** at a marker post. Go through a gate. Spy a windmill to your right. Walk **slightly left** towards a stile continuing in roughly the same direction. Cross the waymarked stile and **walk slightly left** again across a grazing field. In the far corner, go through a gate with a waymarker arrow and walk **straight ahead** to a stile. Cross the stile and walk **straight on** following the hedge. Cross another stile out of the field and walk **straight on** through a copse. Cross yet another stile and walk **straight on** and then **diagonally left** through yet more sheep country to a gate in the far hedge. Go through and cross the lane.

9   Follow the signed footpath **straight ahead** through another gate and onwards. Go through another gate and walk **straight ahead** along the edge of an orchard. Pass a marker post and continue on as both field edge and footpath veer round to the right. Go through a gap in a hedge into an adjoining orchard. Walk **slightly right** but stay to the left of the perpendicular hedge, walking on in roughly the same direction. Pass an HWLT marker post and walk **onwards** and **then left**.

10 **Turn right** in the corner and cross a stile. Walk into a wood. Go through a gate and walk **straight ahead** across a grazing field. At the signpost, **turn left** along recently altered public footpath WC357. Go through a gap in the fence and through a way-marked metal walkers' gate. **Turn right** and walk along the fence. After a while, a large pond, tennis courts and an oast house come into view. Pass a marker post and walk on. Go down a couple of steps, through a metal gate and walk along a small fence.

11 **Turn right** along the signed HWLT. Walk along a track. Pass Dingleden Farm and other buildings. When the cloth industry boomed, this was once the site of fulling mills. Is that a timber-framed barn on the left? Walk up the hill. Pass a signpost and follow the HWLT **straight on** along this easy walking tarmac track. Go **straight ahead** at the first minor T-junction.

12 **Turn left** at the second junction and walk past a postbox. (The Woodcock, a 17th-century pub is further along this lane and may be worth a diversion.) **Turn right** along the signed HWLT immediately after you cross a bridge. Go through a gate and along a pleasant fenced footpath. Go through a gate and **turn left** along the waymarked footpath. Go through another gate and **turn right** along another fenced track. An old stony stretch of path gives a clue there's something special ahead. Go through a gate. This is the 'culvert of Strawberry Wood'. Walk **straight ahead** through the woods on this ancient footpath; keep an eye out for possible 'cobbles' underfoot. Go across a small bridge and through a gate into a field. Walk **diagonally right** up the field ignoring another gate on your right. Climb over a stile in the corner.

Turn right along a fenced mud track and walk up the slope. Continue **straight ahead** through the gate and across the field to go through one final gate. This idyllic grazing field has views back across the Weald and is completed by a shepherd's caravan. A good way to almost finish your walk.

13 Cross the road **with care** and **walk left** along the pavement to return to Benenden.

A TRANQUIL STREAM

13 Orchards & Goudhurst's Stand Against Smugglers

12.4km/7.7miles

A satisfying walk on mainly easy paths through orchards and countryside offering gentle views and an ideally timed, historic lunch stop.

Horsmonden » Grovehurst » Goudhurst » Smallbridge » High Weald Landscape Trail » Horsmonden

Start

Roadside parking in Maidstone Road, Horsmonden, beside the village green and public toilets, opposite the Gun & Spitroast pub. GR: TQ 700405.

The Walk

Horsmonden is on the northern fringes of the High Weald Area of Outstanding Natural Beauty. I initially wanted to include it because of the historic interest of Goudhurst, but after walking this loop, it is equally worthy simply as a delightful walk with some engaging views. The walk passes through several orchards: walking can be a marvellous way to stay in touch with local food sources and seasonal rhythms.

In 1747 there was a 'Magnificent Seven' style showdown in Goudhurst. During the 18th century, a notorious gang of organised criminals, the Hawkhurst Gang, dominated the smuggling trade not just through Romney Marsh but the wider South East. These smugglers used what is now the Star and

Eagle inn by the church, and Spyways, a house on the High Street, for meetings, and demanded help such as horses, goods or money. Powerless locals became so frustrated they formed a vigilante group, the Goudhurst Band of Militia, to defend the village.

The Hawkhurst Gang got wind of this rebellion and vowed revenge, murder and all things grim. Their leader, Thomas Kingsmill, made an 'appointment' to 'sack' the village and murder all inhabitants. On the day in question, the women and children were sent to the next village while the men gathered in the church and a fierce battle was fought. The Hawkhurst Gang weren't expecting resistance and turned tail, and this was perhaps the start of their decline. Spyways is a short distance down the hill on the same side of the road as the pub and the thick oak door is a reminder that this building also once served as the village jail.

ORCHARDS & GOUDHURST'S STAND AGAINST SMUGGLERS

DISTANCE: 12.4KM/7.7MILES » **TOTAL ASCENT**: 244M/799FT » **START GR**: TQ 700405 » **TIME**: ALLOW 3–3.5 HOURS PLUS STOPS » **SATNAV**: TN12 8JJ » **MAP**: OS EXPLORER 136, HIGH WEALD, 1:25,000 » **REFRESHMENTS**: THE GUN & SPITROAST, HORSMONDEN; THE VINE, THE STAR AND EAGLE, AND WEEKS BAKERY AND TEA ROOMS, GOUDHURST » **NAVIGATION**: GENERALLY STRAIGHTFORWARD ALTHOUGH WATCH OUT FOR SEVERAL EASY-TO-MISS TURNS.

13 ORCHARDS & GOUDHURST'S STAND AGAINST SMUGGLERS

Directions – Orchards & Goudhurst's Stand Against Smugglers

⑤ Walk along Maidstone Road and **turn right** and pass the Business Centre and Horsmonden Social Club. In the corner, **walk left** down a twitten past Limes Cottage. **Turn left** along Back Lane and pass the village hall. Cross Orchard Crescent and walk **straight ahead** past the Frances Austen Memorial Hall. Continue **straight ahead** on the signed footpath. Pass some houses and a grazing field.

2 Go **straight ahead** where the footpath forks. Pass an orchard. At the pathway crossroads by the radio transmitter, continue **straight ahead** between the hedges. Pass a waymarked post and continue **diagonally left** across a field. Walk through the birch and hawthorn wind barrier. Go on across the next field and, at the gap in the hedge and waymarked post, cross a small footbridge and go through a metal gate. Walk **straight on** and head towards the **bottom right corner** and go through another metal gate. Walk on along the fenced footpath beside the timber-clad lodge. Climb over a stile. See Grovehurst Lake on your left.

3 **Turn left** on the road for a few steps and **then right** along the signed footpath. Pass some wooden huts and static caravans. Walk on along this easy walking path with fine views.

4 **Turn left** at the corner with the waymarked post and stay on the track. Pass Hurst Cottages where the garden has a sandstone edge. Walk on through the orchards. At the concrete track look for the small gap in the hedge and walk **straight ahead** past the waymarked post.

5 **Easy to miss**: **turn right** at the marker post in front of the distant oast house where the rows of crops end and walk down the hill. Continue past a couple of marker posts. At the bottom of the hill, walk past a third post and follow a waymarked path as it curves right. Cross a footbridge across a wide stream and walk **straight on** along the track. Continue into the next field and pass a waymarked post.

6 Easy to miss: **turn right** at the end of the crop field beside the metal waymarker post and walk along the edge of the field. Pass a marker post and leave the field through a wooden barrier or climb over the old stile. Walk **diagonally right** along a grassy path. Pass a pond and continue on towards an oast house. Walk along a waymarked fence. Emerge opposite Finchurst Granary. **Turn left** along the track. Pass a couple of timber-framed houses.

7 **Turn right** along the busy road **with care** and walk up the hill. Near the top, **turn left** along Gore Lane for about 400m. Pass an oast and various houses.

8 **Turn left** at the footpath sign. Go through the gate and **straight ahead** along the footpath across a field. Climb over a stile and walk along a hedged path. Go down some steps and **turn left** along the track. Pass Swan Farm and continue along a grassy track. Pass a signpost and continue on along the hedge. **Easy to miss: turn right** at the hedge along the unsigned bridleway. Walk down the hill and pass another signpost. **Turn left** at the signpost and walk through the next field. This is the Ladham estate. Walk **straight on** at the next signpost, passing the house.

9 **Turn right** opposite the house to walk along a waymarked hedged track for some way. Emerge on a tarmac lane and follow the signed footpath **straight ahead** to leave the estate.

10 **Turn right** along the lane. Pass Laurel Cottage. Reach the junction at the end of Ladham Road. Cross the busy road (!) and continue along the lane. At the next junction, **turn right** along Tattlebury Lane.

11 At busy Cranbrook Road, **turn right** along the pavement for a few steps. Cross over and **turn left** along the road towards the school but not for long. **Veer left** to continue **straight down** Maypole Lane. **Turn right** opposite the house at an **easy-to-miss** public footpath with an obscured signpost. Climb some steps and go through a kissing gate. Walk across the rough field and enjoy distant views. Pass a charming school allotment, then go through a couple of gates, pass a play area and walk towards the church. The footpath joins the road: **walk left** and then **right** up some steps through the churchyard and then towards the Star and Eagle pub to leave the church. **Walk left** down the High Street.

12   **Turn right** along North Road towards Horsmonden and pass The Vine pub. **Turn left** beside the timber-boarded house to join the signed High Weald Landscape Trail (HWLT). Be careful, the next stretch of footpath is **very steep**. Go through a kissing gate and **take care** down some slippery decking. Go through a kissing gate and across a foot-bridge. Go through another kissing gate and over a small footbridge and **straight on** down a field with far-reaching High Weald views. Walk through one more gate and footbridge and continue down to the corner of the field. Go through a kissing gate and along a fenced track with several more kissing gates.

13   Cross the lane and climb over a waymarked stile. Walk through a field and cross another stile. **Turn left** to walk about 1.6km along the lane, still following the HWLT. Walk past various houses. Walk up the hill and pass Park Farm house. At the junction, **cross the first lane** to the traffic island and **veer left** along the road. Pass Rectory Park. Look back and see Goudhurst on the hill.

14   **Turn right** along the signed HWLT and public footpath and go through the kissing gate. Walk **straight ahead** past the dead tree and on through the grazing field. Go through a kissing gate in the far corner. Walk down the hill past some impressive oak trees. Head **diagonally right** towards the end of the fence, past a gate and a clump of trees. Walk through a waymarked kissing gate and across a walkers' footbridge. Walk **straight on** up the next field to a kissing gate. Walk on towards a big oak near a hut. Go through a kissing gate and along a fenced footpath. Walk **straight ahead** past a stable and through a kissing gate.

15   Cross the lane and walk **straight ahead** along a tarmac byway towards Cherry View. Pass a bungalow and walk on along a hedged section. At the field see a waymarker arrow and the telegraph post and **turn left** to walk along the edge. Cross a footbridge and stay on this path until you reach the road. At Horsmonden, cross the street and **turn left** to return to the village green.

ROLLING FIELDS & HIGH WEALD VIEWS

DISTANCE: 16.4KM/10.2MILES » **TOTAL ASCENT**: 271M/888FT » **START GR**: TQ 882333 » **TIME**: ALLOW 4–4.5 HOURS PLUS STOPS » **SATNAV**: TN30 6HN » **MAP**: OS EXPLORER 125, ROMNEY MARSH, RYE & WINCHELSEA, 1:25,000 » **REFRESHMENTS**: THE EWE & LAMB, ROLVENDEN LAYNE; THE BULL INN, ROLVENDEN; HOLE PARK GARDENS TEA ROOMS OPEN SELECTED DAYS; LOTS OF CHOICE IN TENTERDEN INCLUDING A GOOD FISH AND CHIP SHOP BESIDE THE CAR PARK » **NAVIGATION**: STRAIGHTFORWARD EXCEPT FOR AMBIGUOUS SECTIONS IN POINTS 3 AND 4.

VIEW ACROSS A WHEAT FIELD

14 Rolling Fields & High Weald Views

16.4km/10.2miles

From Tenterden Museum along peaceful paths through the agricultural High Weald past oast and timber-boarded houses, with refreshments stops and settlements to explore.

Tenterden » Halden Place » Hole Park » Rolvenden » Rolvenden Layne » High Weald Landscape Trail » Tenterden

Start

Station Road (paid) car park, Tenterden. Close to public toilets and Tenterden Museum. GR: TQ 882333.

The Walk

Tenterden is a place where you might pleasantly while away some time. This small town began life as a clearing in the forest of Anderida, providing acorns to fatten pigs but, later, the town thrived as a weaving centre and was also known for shipbuilding, supplying ships and men against French raiders. Its fortunes faltered when the ports were silted up and plans for a railway failed. Tenterden Museum is open seasonally with a small admission charge and is a good starting point to learn more about the story of Cinque Ports.

This trail twice crosses the Kent & East Sussex Railway and you will see and hear steam trains if they're running. Otherwise, this walk tends to be peaceful. It's an agricultural area so expect to cross grazing pastures and crop fields, and to weave your way past barns and oast houses.

Hole Park Gardens are open on selected days, with home-made teas and light lunches served in the Coach House. The Bull Inn at Rolvenden could be a good place to stop for lunch, or push on a little further and The Ewe & Lamb offers 'snacks' which are sure to fuel your remaining steps. In Rolvenden, you can't miss imposing St Mary the Virgin church, largely unchanged since 1480.

The last part of this route follows a pleasant section of the High Weald Landscape Trail through crop fields and on wooded paths. It passes Great Maytham Hall where novelist Frances Hodgson Burnett lived from 1898 to 1907. Its walled garden provided the inspiration for the much-loved children's story *The Secret Garden*. Burnett wrote the story after discovering a neglected walled garden. She found a door hidden amongst the ivy, and began the restoration of the garden, which she planted with hundreds of roses. She set up a table and chair in the gazebo, and, dressed always in a white dress and large hat, wrote a number of books in the peace and tranquillity of her scented secret garden.

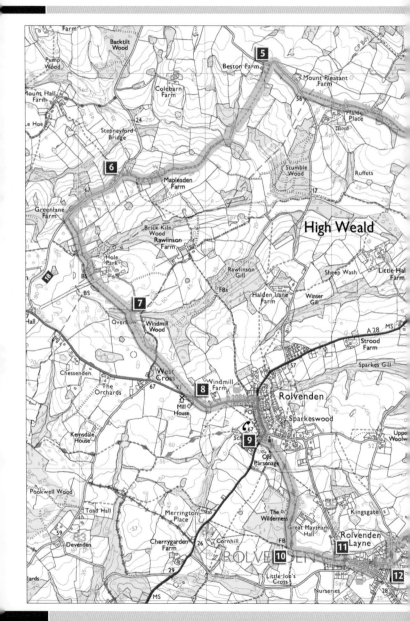

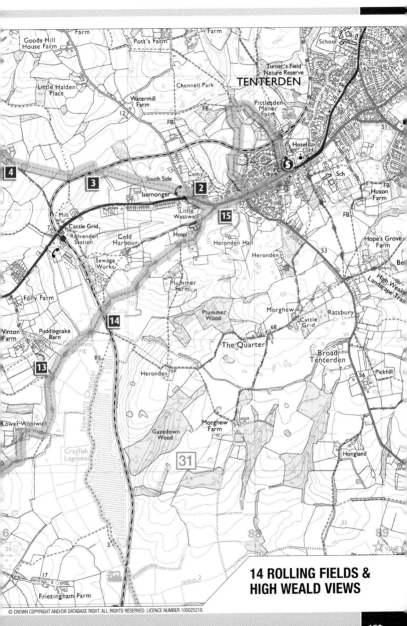

14 ROLLING FIELDS & HIGH WEALD VIEWS

Directions – Rolling Fields & High Weald Views

⊕ **Turn left** out of Station Road car park and walk down the hill towards Kent & East Sussex Railway. Walk past the entrance to Tenterden Town station and cross the railway line. The driveway forks: walk to the **right** of the large tree towards a yellow waymarker emblem on a gatepost. Walk on through or round the vehicle gates to the K&ESR car park. Go **straight ahead**, leaving the concrete sleeper path and head for another yellow waymarker on a gatepost. Walk **slightly left** across the stream and follow the clear pathway along the hedge and fence.

At the kissing gate, **walk left** a few steps on the public footpath along the edge of the field. Look out for a waymarked post. **Turn left** through this second metal kissing gate. Walk through the gap at the end of the fence and continue on to pass another waymarked post. Walk towards the gatepost to the right of the distant church tower but, just before it, **turn right** through a waymarked kissing gate. Walk towards the railway signal. **Take care** and follow the instructions to use this open crossing.

Go through the gate and walk **straight on** through the gap. (A waymarker post was broken at time of writing.) Walk **straight on** along the trees up the slope. Pass a dilapidated iron shed and a waymarked wooden gatepost. Walk on along beside the fence. Pass Garden Cottage and walk on along the driveway. Walk **straight on** to the end of West Cross Gardens. **Turn right** along the High Street. On the opposite side of the road, pass the William Caxton pub and the stone gate to Heronden Hall. Cross Westwell Court. Continue out of town. At Westwell House entrance, **stay on the grass verge** to walk past the waymarker signpost and along the footpath beside the wall. Watch out: slippery stones underfoot.

2 **Turn right** at Cranbrook Road for a few steps and **then left** through a gate along the signed public footpath. Walk **diagonally right** across the grazing field. Climb over a stile. Continue in the same **diagonally right** direction to the field corner. Climb over a stile and walk along the fence.

3 Cross at the railway crossing following instructions on boards. Close the gates and then cross the footbridge and **turn left**. Follow the stream along to a stile in the nearby corner. Cross the double stile and footbridge. **Take care** here: the second stile is currently broken (2018) so the waymarker is hard to read and the path is otherwise unsigned. Walk **straight on** across the field on the footpath and go through the gate. Continue

straight ahead up the slope towards the left-hand side of the barns. Go through the gate and on up the field to go through a smaller metal gate. **Turn left** for a few steps.

4 **Turn right** along the bridleway, passing the tile-hung house. Walk through some farm buildings and past a white house. The footpath continues along the side of a crop field with fine views to an oast house on the right. Follow the track on past a white timber-boarded house. The path becomes concrete and passes through more farm buildings. **Turn right** through the waymarked gate, turning away from red-brick Halden Place. Walk along the concrete bridleway beside a crop field; in the next field the footpath runs diagonally left but, because of the crops, it can be **tricky to locate exactly**: you need to **head left** and up towards the kissing gate in the top left corner. Go through the gate and **turn right** along the lane. Occasional cars!

5 **Turn left** through a kissing gate just before you reach the oast house. You are entering Hole Park estate. Follow the signed footpath along the edge of the field. Go through the next kissing gate and walk **straight ahead** next to the fence. After the waymarked fencepost walk to the **right** of the large clump of trees. Walk **diagonally right** towards the gate. By a marker post, go through the wooden gate. Walk **diagonally right** on the waymarked footpath **straight ahead**. About two thirds of the way down, look for a way-marked kissing gate on the right-hand side of the field. Go through and walk **diagonally left**. Go through another kissing gate, across a footbridge and walk along a hedged footpath. Emerge from this wooded path and **walk straight ahead** through some farm buildings. Walk past an oast house and then through a gate and past some more houses.

6 **Turn left** and climb up the lane. After approx. 500m **turn left** at the signposted footpath. Go through a kissing gate into Hole Park estate. Walk **straight ahead** along the left-hand side of the hedge. At the gap, spot a waymarked arrow and walk past the post, continuing **straight ahead**. Pass a fenced plantation area. Walk across a tarmac drive with a *Private* sign and, at the path junction, without going through the gates, **keep left** along the grassy path, continuing in roughly the same direction along the laurel hedge. At the end, walk **straight on** through a timber yard and **turn left** through the wide gap towards a big house. Hole Park Gardens are open on selected days when the Coach House cafe is open too. **Walk right** on the waymarked footpath. With the entrance on your right, go **straight ahead** through a small gate in the metal fence. Walk **diagonally left** through a grazing field to another small metal gate on the far edge.

7   **Walk diagonally left** and over a foot plank between two fishing ponds. Go through a kissing gate and walk **diagonally left**. Climb on up the slope passing a war memorial on the far side of the field. Pass a marker on the fence. Walk **diagonally left** and pass a marooned stile and marker post. Follow the footpath up in the rough direction of the windmill. Just beyond the mill and the house, at the end of the hedge, go through a kissing gate.

8   **Turn left** along the footpath by the road and walk to Rolvenden. Walk past the park and The Bull Inn. **Turn right** along Rolvenden High Street. Pass the general stores and The Star pub. Stay on the main road where it bends right at the junction.

9   **Turn left** along Church Row to join the signed High Weald Landscape Trail (HWLT). **Keep left** on the brick path through the churchyard, **ignoring** the offshoot path to a metal gate. Leave the brick path at the curve to keep walking in the same direction on the mud footpath to a wooden kissing gate. Go through and follow the HWLT **diagonally left**. You are staying on the HWLT for the remainder of this walk so look out for emblems. This grassy path wends through grazing fields through one gap in the hedge and then another with a waymarked post. Go **straight ahead** and see a pond off down to the right. Go through a waymarked gate and follow a wooded, easy path along a fence. Pass a gravel car park and catch a glimpse of Great Maytham Hall as you proceed along the path. Go through a kissing gate.

10   **Turn left** following the HWLT. From here, there's a good view of Great Maytham Hall, inspiration for *The Secret Garden*. Go through the gate and continue **straight ahead**, following the HWLT along the edge of the field. Go through another kissing gate and walk along a narrow fenced path. Pass a pond. Go through another kissing gate and walk **straight on**. Go through a gate.

11   This is Rolvenden Layne. We leave the HWLT briefly to divert past a pub. **Walk right** along Maytham Road to the Ewe & Lamb. Return to the HWLT by the footpath at the pub's side and **turn right** on Frensham Road.

12   **Turn left** along Mounts Lane following the HWLT. **Turn right** through the gate at the waymarker signpost following the HWLT. **Keep left** at the gate. Walk through the crop field. Pass a marker post and continue on the other side of the hedgerow. **Turn left** down some waymarked steps. Pass another marker post and walk **diagonally right** through a crop field. **Turn right** along the edge at the marker post. **Turn left** through the kissing gate and walk **right**, along the hedgerow. In the next field, **turn left** at the marker post and walk up towards the house. At the top, pass a waymarked post and go up a couple of steps. **Turn right** along the mud track and HWLT. Pass the timber-framed barn, house and oast house. Follow the mud track along a hedge and walk most of the hedge way down the slope. **Easy to miss**: **turn left** through a waymarked narrow gap in the hedge, opposite a mud footpath cutting through the crops. Walk on along the footpath through the crops. **Walk left** at the rough grass, along the edge of the crops. **Turn right** at the marker post. Pass a marker post and cross a footbridge. Walk on.

13   At the footpath junction and signpost, walk **straight on** for a while. Pass a marker post and walk **diagonally left**. Hear or see steam trains! Cross a bridge over a stream and walk **diagonally left** past an HWLT marker post on the footpath.

14   Use the railway crossing **with care**. Walk **diagonally left** away from the track to cross a footbridge. Follow the HWLT **right** on the footpath. Go back across another foot-bridge and **walk left** and along the hedge on the HWLT. At the end, **turn left** passing an HWLT marker stump. Walk past some fallen tree trunks. **Turn right** across a stile in the corner and follow the waymarked path **diagonally left** across the field. Go through a metal gate and walk along a wooded path. **Walk left** at the lane, following the HWLT arrow. Follow the lane round as it curves right.

15   **Turn right** and cross the road to walk along the High Street. **Turn left** down Station Road to return to your car.

BEWL WATER FROM THE OPTIONAL ROUTE TO COUSLEY WOOD

15 A Loop Around Bewl Water

20.3km/12.6miles

A deservedly popular lakeside loop, ideal for those seeking fitness and relaxation, with diversions that add interest and pub options.

Bewl Water Visitor Centre » Sussex Border Path » Bewl Water Woods » Birchett's Green » Tolhurst » Boarder's Bridge » Dunsters Bay » Sussex Border Path » Bewl Water Visitor Centre

Start

All-day (paid) parking at Bewl Water. Check www.bewlwater.co.uk for latest information. GR: TQ 675338.

The Walk

A walk around Bewl Water provides the opportunity to walk in the countryside without the worry of negotiating farm livestock or more intricate trails. At 12.6 miles, this circuit makes for a good day's walk, and is within the reach of many of moderate fitness. If you don't have the time or inclination to do the whole trail, Bewl Water may offer a water taxi service; you can find the latest details on their website (**www.bewlwater.co.uk**). You will notice two main climbs, around Birchett's Green and Tolhurst, but they are on easy surfaces. Overall, the route is a mixture of well-surfaced bridleways, grassy waterside footpaths, tranquil lanes and woodland tracks. Take a picnic, divert under a mile to the 14th-century Bull Inn at Ticehurst or, if you don't mind a bit more of a walk, enjoy views over the reservoir as you climb to The Old Vine Inn at Cousley Wood. The cafe at the visitor centre can be a welcome sight too.

Today, Bewl Water is valued for its beauty, the water it supplies to Medway towns and, of course, the recreational opportunities for walkers, fishermen, cyclists and boaters, but, back in the 1970s, how did people feel when a dam was built to create this huge reservoir? This was not a densely populated area and disruption was minimal but, in all, eleven buildings and several lanes were submerged. Farmers relocated stock and properties. Tindalls Cottage, the 18th-century home of a labourer, was painstakingly moved to the Weald and Downland Living Museum, while 14th-century Dunsters Mill House was moved half a mile up the hill. Landscapes often indicate history but this change was so immense, it's hard to see what once was where now there is water.

A LOOP AROUND BEWL WATER

DISTANCE: 20.3KM/12.6MILES » TOTAL ASCENT: 424M/1,392FT » START GR: TQ 675338 » TIME: ALLOW 6 HOURS PLUS STOPS » SATNAV: TN3 8JH » MAP: OS EXPLORER 136, HIGH WEALD, 1:25,000 » REFRESHMENTS: WATERFRONT CAFE AND KIOSK AT BEWL WATER VISITOR CENTRE; THE BULL INN, TICEHURST; THE OLD VINE INN, COUSLEY WOOD » NAVIGATION: STRAIGHTFORWARD BUT CHECK DIRECTIONS AND MAP TO AVOID MISTAKES. BEWL MARKER POSTS: OUR DISTANCES REFER TO AMOUNT WALKED RATHER THAN MILES TO GO.

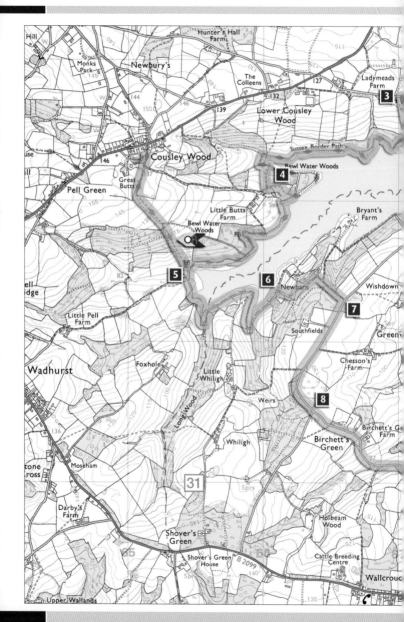

15 A LOOP AROUND BEWL WATER

Directions – A Loop Around Bewl Water

➎ Turn left along the tarmac road above the visitor centre. Walk through a metal gate and, at the junction, **turn left** towards the signed exit. **Walk right** at the Boat House Bistro fork and notice the Round Bewl Water route blue bridleway arrow on the marker post. Walk up the hill away from the gates.

2 **Turn left** along Bewlbridge Lane to follow the Round Bewl Water route.

3 **Turn left** into Hook Hill Lane, following the brown Bewl Water loop sign. Walk down the hill and follow the blue arrows as the bridleway curves right. Stay on this lane and pass a white barrier. Walk past a wooden gate and **turn right** along the bridleway: keep the water on your left as you walk through the woods. Pass a marker post and enjoy the views as the landscape opens out. Climb steadily and walk through more woods on the gravel bridleway.

4 **Turn right** at the stile before Frogwell Wood. Walk up beside the border of the field and woods on the footpath. At the signpost, **turn right** to walk between the fences on the permissive footpath. Go through a kissing gate. **Turn left** along the footpath passing Bewl Water oast and a signpost. Walk past a wide waymarked gate and continue along the footpath. **Turn left** at the signpost. Walk past the hay barns and through a waymarked gap in the fence to continue along a narrow track. At the walkers' gate, **turn right** along the bridleway and walk on through the woodland.

5 To continue around Bewl Water, walk **straight ahead** at the wooden signpost* and path junction, staying on the bridleway up a slight hill and onwards through the woods. Pass the Bewl *3 miles* marker point and enjoy stretches of open path and woodland.

> **OR** *At the signpost, **turn right** to walk just over 800m to the 16th-century pub, The Old Vine at Cousley Wood. Climb over a stile and follow the Sussex Border Path **straight ahead** and then **slightly diagonally left** up a steepish slope towards the corner. Climb over a stile and walk **straight ahead** along the left-hand edge of the field. At the top, **turn left** at a marker post and walk along the field edge and up to a signpost by a gap in the hedge. Continue along a mud track. **Turn left** along a lane. At the road, **turn left** to walk a few steps to the pub. Retrace your steps to rejoin the main route.

6   At the brown sign, **turn right** following the signed Bewl Water route up the slope. **Turn right** to walk up the lane and bridleway. Walk **straight ahead** past a signpost and brown Bewl Water sign.

7   **Turn right** following the brown Round Bewl Water sign and arrows. Walk **straight on** at the junction passing an **easy-to-miss** wooden Round Bewl Water marker post on your right.

8   **Turn left** up the road at the T-junction following the brown Bewl Water route sign. Pass The Oast and Birchett's Green Farmhouse. Continue on. Pass Birchett's Point. Continue past some houses and up the lane. Climb the hill and pass Quarry Farm.

9   **Turn left** at the T-junction at the top of Birchett's Green Lane following the brown Bewl Water route signs. Walk down the hedged lane passing several houses.

10   At the junction beside the Southern Water Nature Reserve gate, you have a choice:

To continue around Bewl, walk **straight on** following the brown Bewl Water route. Pass a pond and some houses. Walk **straight ahead** through the gates. Note the marker post: you have now walked 7 miles (and have about 6 to go!). Keep walking along the path, enjoying the watery views and peaceful atmosphere. Go over a foot-bridge and follow the blue waymarker arrows **straight ahead** up the steps. Pass a house and walk along the fence.

> **OR** Or **turn right** to walk just under 800m along the lane to visit The Bull Inn. From the pub, **turn left** along the lane and **keep left** at the fork. At the sign-post, **turn left** along a footpath which soon curves to the right past a marker post. Walk on along this pleasant footpath until you reach the cattle grid and signpost. **Turn right** and rejoin the Round Bewl Water circuit at Point 11.

11   Cross the drive following the Round Bewl Water signs. **Turn right** along the bridleway at the gate following the Round Bewl Water route through the woods. Pass the *5 miles to go* marker post. Walk on along the path. Pass a marker post and **head right** as waymarked.

Turn left along the Round Bewl Water route, as signed. Pass a car park at Dunsters Bay (and Mill House) and walk round the gate. Follow the bridleway. Walk **straight on** past a signpost and more importantly a *4 miles to go* post! Continue on for nearly half a mile. Walk **straight on** past a signpost in the woods and continue along this easy path. Pass a *3 miles to go* post! Go through a gate.

12 Turn left along a lane following the Round Bewl Water arrow and walk across the bridge. **Turn left** along the path following the Round Bewl Water route arrow. Pass Rosemary Farmhouse and go through the waymarked gate. Walk along the banks of the reservoir on the path. Note the oast house on the far shore. Keep walking! Pass through a wooded area. Walk across the bridge over the creek. Pass the *2 miles to go* post! Walk on through the woods and stay on the bridleway. You are nearly there! Pass the *1 mile to go* post. Walk **straight on** through a gate.

13 Walk left across the dam. Follow the path into the trees and up some steps. The second flight of wooden steps leads to the cafe and car park.

THE RESERVOIR

Saxon Shore & 1066 Country

This iconic area attracts tourists but its stalwart shoreline may surprise locals too. The little-known coves of Hastings Country Park are a delight. Our walk around Battle invites you to tramp across hills and through woods, past thousand-year-old yew trees and historic churches, to imagine the landscape around the 1066 battlefield. Bodiam Castle, Salehurst and Smallhythe Place were all built beside rivers and have stories to tell. Our expansive waterways route explores the changing fortunes of the Rother Valley and how our 'Saxon Shore' left places like the 'Isle of Oxney' exposed to plunder. Near Rye, our simple trail passes bird haven Cadborough Cliff and climbs to an ancient settlement before returning along the river through sheep-farming country. Meander through woodlands, along wild riverbanks and soak up myriad views. You won't be disappointed.

RIVER ROTHER (ROUTE 16)

CADBOROUGH CLIFF, TILLINGHAM VALLEY & RYE

DISTANCE: 12.1KM/7.5MILES » **TOTAL ASCENT**: 133M/437FT » **START GR**: TQ 917202 » **TIME**: ALLOW 2.5–3 HOURS PLUS STOPS » **SATNAV**: TN31 7EL » **MAP**: OS EXPLORER 125, ROMNEY MARSH, RYE & WINCHELSEA, 1:25,000 » **REFRESHMENTS**: THE HORSE & CART INN, PEASMARSH (WALKER AND DOG FRIENDLY. GARDEN); VARIOUS OPTIONS IN RYE » **NAVIGATION**: BE CAREFUL AT THE HAMMONDS. OTHERWISE STRAIGHTFORWARD.

THE CHALK PATH AT CADBOROUGH CLIFF

16 Cadborough Cliff, Tillingham Valley & Rye

12.1km/7.5miles

A wildlife-rich stroll beside Cadborough Cliff, sheep-farming country, a friendly pub and an ancient approach to Rye along the river.

Rye » Cadborough Cliff » Pelsham » Peasmarsh » High Weald Landscape Trail » River Tillingham » Rye

Start

Riverside parking, Winchelsea Road opposite Rye Heritage Centre. Start point by the bridge. GR: TQ 917202. Alternative start at Gibbet Marsh, by Point 2. GR: TQ 914202, TN31 7DT.

The Walk

The walk begins with a marvellous stretch of the 1066 Country Walk: enjoy chalk beneath your feet and the scent of rambling briars, although Cadborough Cliff may not be quite what you expect. The stream is quiet but the scrubby abundance of the grassy slopes provides lush sustenance for wildlife and, if you are fortunate, an orchestra may tune up to see you on your way: blackbird, song thrush, chaffinch, chiffchaff, blackcap, whitethroat, reed warbler or wren; it's hard to distinguish the calls but then comes the distinctive purr of a turtledove. It is an undoubted privilege to hear this increasingly rare bird.

There are intermittent climbs along the way, but as a reward, you can enjoy cooling hilltop breezes and views over the wind farm and Rye harbour, the Tillingham valley, the Rother valley, oast houses and grazing pastures.

This is sheep-farming country; footpaths are a mixture of hedged and open tracks but dogs need to be under close control if not on the lead. There are many easy walking bridleways which serve occasional large houses as driveways.

The church of St Peter and St Paul at Peasmarsh dates form 1070 and is known for its excellent acoustics. Much of the original church remains, including the Norman chancel arch. This hilltop site was once the Anglo-Saxon settlement of Tetbald and some evidence of Roman occupation exists. The settlement was perhaps abandoned due to an outbreak of the plague in the 14th century.

You too can head for modern-day Peasmarsh if you wish to visit the pub. The tree-lined track back to Rye through aptly named Sheepfold has a time-worn feel too. Rye lies ahead; a castle and medieval port on a hilltop and the blue sea by its side.

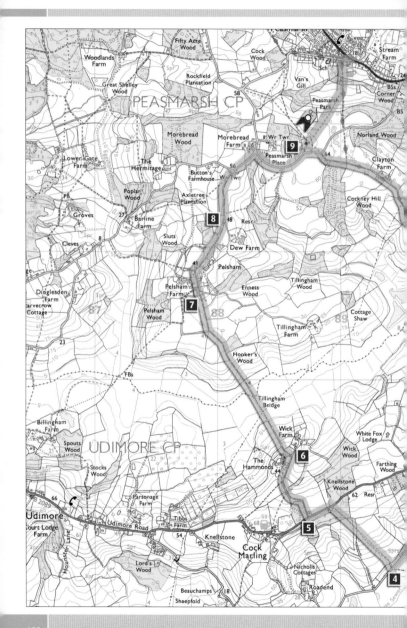

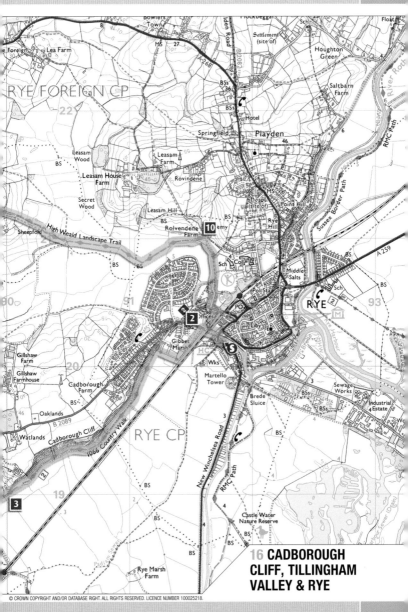

RYE FOREIGN CP

High Weald Landscape Trail

Sheepfold

Cadborough Cliff

1066 Country Walk

RYE CP

New Winchelsea Road

RMC Path

Gillshaw Farm

Gillshaw Farmhouse

Cadborough Farm

Oaklands

Watlands

B 2089

Bowlers Town

Rye Foreign

Lea Farm

Settlement (site of)

Houghton Green

Saltbarn Farm

Hotel

Springfield

Playden

Leasam Wood

Leasam Farm

Leasam House Farm

Rovindene

Secret Wood

Leasam Hill

Rolvendene Farm

Point Hill

Rye Hill

Sussex Border Path

RMC Path

River Rother

Sch

Middle Salts

RYE

Sewage Works

Brede Sluice

Martello Tower

Gibbet Marsh

Wks

Industrial Estate

Castle Water Nature Reserve

Rye Marsh Farm

16 CADBOROUGH CLIFF, TILLINGHAM VALLEY & RYE

Directions – Cadborough Cliff, Tillingham Valley & Rye

➎ By the pedestrian crossing at the bridge, there are signposted footpaths on both sides of the river. Take the **left-hand** path, following the waymarked 1066 Country Walk (1066 CW) across the pedestrian railway crossing. See the windmill on the far bank.

2 **Turn left** at the clearing along the tarmac path. Cross a footbridge and initially follow the cycle path. Pass National Cycle Network 2 markers and some houses. Walk past a red-brick waterworks and go through a metal gate along the waymarked footpath. Look out for the red 1066 CW marker posts. The path becomes more chalky. After some way, pass through a gate.

3 Continue **straight ahead** at the house with the flagpole. Go through the gate and walk **straight ahead** along the narrow (!) lower lane. At the road junction, walk **straight ahead** along Float Lane (!).

4 **Turn right** at the signposted gate following the waymarked footpath. Almost immediately climb over a stile and follow the signed footpath **ahead** and climb steeply through the crop field. Continue in a straight line through a gap in the hedge and along the (unmarked) footpath, across one stile, and then over another, marked *Footpath*. Walk through Knellstone Wood. **Turn left** along the road.

5 At Wick Farm, cross the road and **turn right** along the signed bridleway.

6 **Turn left** at the bridleway signpost at The Hammonds. **Careful here!** Leave the tarmac drive after 50m, where it curves, and walk **straight ahead**, along the fence to a not-obvious gate. Go through and continue **straight ahead** on the bridleway to walk down the field and through a couple of gates and fields. Cross a waymarked footbridge. Go through one gate and then another, **keeping right** along the fenced track. Climb the hill. Go through a gate and follow the track. It runs between hedges and undulates.

7 Emerge at Pelsham Farm Cottage on a lane. Walk **straight ahead** up the hill. Pass some large houses. Follow the lane and bridleway as it curves right and onwards. Pass Pelsham house and hedged grounds. See a pond on your left. Pass through some large, open gates.

8 **Turn left** along the lane/ bridleway and walk on along this easy walking surface, keeping your height. At the road, **go right**, walking in the same direction. Pass Dew Cottage. **Turn right** at the next junction towards Rye. Pass Peasmarsh Place care home. There may be more cars now.

9 Arrive at the hilltop church of St Peter and St Paul and explore the churchyard, site of an ancient settlement.

> Optional route to The Horse & Cart pub, Peasmarsh. **Turn left** at the church following the signed footpath to Peasmarsh. Walk past the church and through the kissing gate in a corner of the churchyard. **Walk left** and then **right** around the edge of the field, passing a pond. Follow the footpath through the crop field. Climb over a stile and follow the footpath **diagonally right**. At the bottom, cross a couple of stiles. Cross one last stile and arrive in Peasmarsh. **Turn right** for the pub. Retrace your footsteps back up and through the churchyard.

Leave the church and **turn left** along the road. At Clayton Farm, **turn right** along the signed public bridleway, passing the orchards. At the marker post, walk **straight ahead** on the bridleway. The High Weald Landscape Trail (HWLT) joins us here. Follow the track through some buildings and then down a tree-lined track. Go through a gate and follow the bridleway straight ahead. At the bridleway post walk **straight ahead**. Go through the waymarked gate, following the footpath **straight ahead**. At the bottom of the field, cross the walkers' footbridge and walk **straight ahead**. At the end of the next field, walk through a gate. Follow the bridleway **straight ahead** and head for the gate some way to the left of the river. Go through a waymarked gate, following the HWLT **straight ahead**. Follow the river round to the left. Go through the gate and follow the HWLT **right**.

10 At Rolvendene Farm, pass the marker post and follow the HWLT **right** along the course of the river. Go through a gate and **walk right** along a tarmac path, arriving in town. Follow the path until you emerge at the Queen Adelaide. Cross the road and walk **straight ahead**. Pass the fire station and follow the narrow track along the side of the windmill. **Turn left** through the gate and cross the pedestrian railway crossing and continue. Emerge at the bridge opposite the car park.

ST MARY THE VIRGIN CHURCH IN SALEHURST

17 Along the River of Time to Bodiam Castle

13km/8.1miles

A historic loop along the Rother valley joining settlements, abbey, castle and church.

Robertsbridge » Robertsbridge Abbey » Bodiam » Salehurst » The Clappers » Robertsbridge

Start

Robertsbridge Station car park, Station Road. GR: TQ 734234. Alternative parking at Robertsbridge (Station Road) car park – long stay on Sundays only. GR: TQ 737235.

The Walk

The name of Robertsbridge is first mentioned in a 13th-century abbey document which refers to *Pons Roberti*. The oldest known house in the village is dated circa 1390 and can still be seen as numbers 1–4 Fair Lane on the first part of our trail. Later, walk past the abbey, a listed farmhouse which incorporates parts of what would once have been the Abbot's house, originally built in time for a visit by Henry III. The abbey came to an end as part of the Dissolution of the Monasteries. In the garden, glimpse the ruins of this Cistercian abbey's refectory. The river retains the timeless feel of a track well trodden.

Arrive at the bridge in Bodiam, constructed on the site of a Roman road. The present bridge was built in 1797 for the county of Sussex by Richard Louch for the princely sum of £1,150 and has been recently restored. Bodiam embodies romanticised notions of a castle with its spiral staircases, battlements and a portcullis, but it's very much a castle in a wider landscape too and, as you walk, it's easy to imagine the role of the river and these footpaths in the lives of ordinary people. Glimpse its exterior from a public footpath or choose to explore this renowned National Trust property more fully.

The Domesday Book describes Salehurst settlement as having '*7 villagers and 8 cottagers, with 6 ploughs, a church and 16 acres*'. In St Mary's church, the font is rumoured to have been a gift from King Richard the Lionheart in thanks to the abbey for helping to raise his ransom when captured on the Crusades.

ALONG THE RIVER OF TIME TO BODIAM CASTLE

DISTANCE: 13KM/8.1MILES » **TOTAL ASCENT**: 124M/407FT » **START GR**: TQ 734234 » **TIME**: ALLOW 3 HOURS PLUS STOPS **MAP**: OS EXPLORER 136, HIGH WEALD, 1:25,000 » **SATNAV**: TN32 5DD » **REFRESHMENTS**: THE GEORGE INN, ROBERTSBRIDGE; CASTLE INN, AND NT WHARF TEA ROOM, BODIAM; THE SALEHURST HALT, SALEHURST » **NAVIGATION**: TAKE CARE AT POINTS 4, 5 AND 8; CONSULT DIRECTIONS AND MAP POINTS.

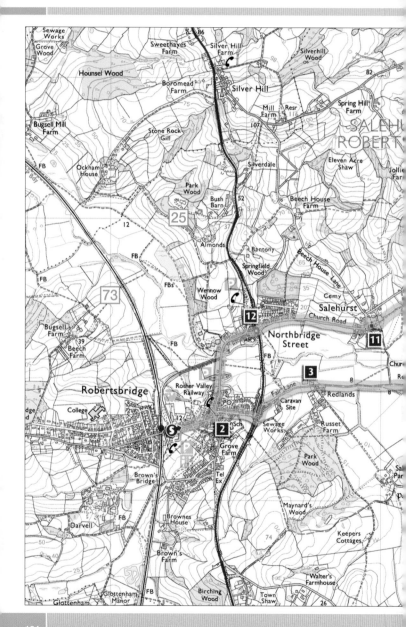

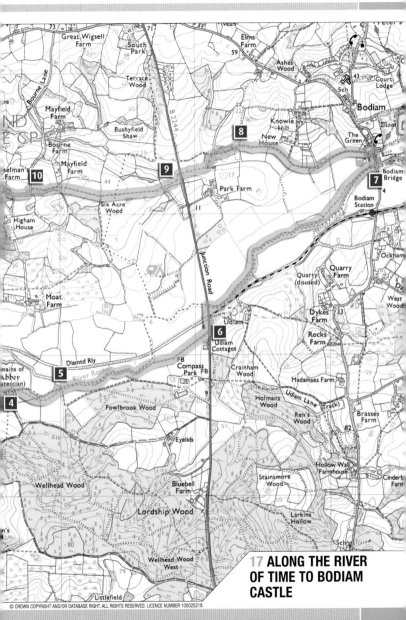

17 ALONG THE RIVER OF TIME TO BODIAM CASTLE

Directions – Along the River of Time to Bodiam Castle

⮕ Exit the car park and **turn left** past the Ostrich hotel. Pass Willowbank and walk over the bridge. Pass the village shop, Robertsbridge Club, public toilets and alternative parking at Station Road car park. Walk to the end of the road.

2 **Turn left** at the High Street. Cross and, almost immediately, **turn right** along Fair Lane. Walk along and pass a signed footpath and fenced park and then pass cul-de-sac Fayre Meadow. Continue **straight ahead** along the signed bridleway and across a footbridge over the busy A21. **Turn left** after the bridge and walk along the wooded path up above the road for a short distance. **Turn right** and walk along the lane. Glimpse Salehurst to your left.

3 At the oast house and junction, walk **straight ahead** on the bridleway. Pass a *Private Road No Vehicle Access* sign and walk on along the bridleway towards Greyfriars Farm. Walk **straight on** past a signpost, following the easy walking bridleway. Pass an oast house and the abbey (now a private house but you can glimpse the ruins in the garden).

4 Walk **straight ahead** along the unsigned footpath (leaving the bridleway which is signed right). Walk past a gate. Fifty metres ahead, reach a waymarker signpost beside a stile. Climb over and follow the footpath across the field. Cross the next (currently broken) stile and **walk right** along the waymarked, fenced, footpath. At the end of the fence, walk **straight on**.

5 **Easy to miss**: the footpath forks here. **Turn left** at a marker-posted gap in the fence to walk up and along the riverbanks. (You need to turn **before** the clear signpost which is the other fork.) Walk along the riverbank and cross a small footbridge. Enjoy this peaceful path. Cross a longer footbridge. See an old railway bridge to your left. Walk on past a brick pillbox and marker post. Walk **straight ahead** across the field on the waymarked footpath. Pass a signpost to your right and beyond it see a large modern building which may provide a useful landmark later. Climb over the stile beside the road bridge over the stream.

6 Turn left along the road. **Take care**: no verge for 50m. Cross over near Udiam Farm and walk along the grass verge but **ignore** a milestone and waymarked gate. Cross the bridge over the river. **Turn right** at the signpost and wide gateway. Follow the footpath to walk between crops and riverbank. You may see or hear intermittent puffs and hoots from the Rother Valley Railway on the other side of the river. Continue along the riverbank for some way. Pass the Hub cafe and canoe hire on the opposite bank. As you approach Bodiam, look out for the castle battlements on the horizon.

7 Arrive at the bridge in Bodiam. Cross the road and **turn left** for a step or two. **Turn right** through the gateway if you wish to explore Bodiam castle. Pass between the cafe and shop. Public toilets on left. Visiting the castle is highly recommended if time allows. Exit and cross the road. **Turn left** at the signpost just past the Castle Inn. Walk along the tarmac footpath past the cricket ground and vineyards. Continue past a metal gate. **Keep left** at the fork by the marker post: **careful** – the inclination is to walk right here. Walk along the easy walking pubic footpath. The path runs beside a stream. Go through a gate.

8 **Now this is tricky**. There's a notice on the marker post to your right and a green barn on your left. Continue **straight ahead** through the gap between gate and marker post to continue along the tarmac footpath and track through the warehouses and Brentwood House. **Turn left** at the signpost to cross the footbridge towards the pond. Walk past the picnic tables until you're almost at the far end of the pond. Take a few steps **right** after the fence to walk on along the footpath. **Turn right** at the signpost in the field. Cross a stile and head **diagonally left** to the gate on to the road. Cross this fast road carefully.

9 Climb over the stile and **head left** up the hill. See a waymarker arrow stuck on a tree and **turn right** across the field. Climb over the stile and follow the signed footpath **straight ahead**, looking for the well-trodden grass path. Pass to the **right** of a clump of trees. The River Rother, out of sight, and the large modern building you passed earlier are on your distant left. Keep going in the same direction as before, and, as you approach the trees, a gap becomes visible. Climb over the stile and follow the signed footpath **straight ahead** up the grazing field. Go through an open gate with a waymarker arrow on the other side. Continue **straight on** towards the telegraph pole at the edge of the field and in front of the houses. Climb over the stile.

Directions – Along the River of Time to Bodiam Castle continued...

10 **Walk left** along the narrow lane (!). Pass several houses. **Turn left** at the milestone, go through the gate and walk **straight ahead** to the stepping stones and along the wall, respecting this private garden. Follow the footpath along the fence, keeping the pond on your left until you go through the gate. **Turn right** following the waymarked arrows and then **immediately left** at the marker post. Go through the gate and **walk left** along the edge of the field. Go through the next gate and continue **straight ahead** past the fruit trees. Walk on between two waymarked fences. Go through a gate and **turn right** along the driveway and footpath. Walk to the signpost where you **head right** to cross the waymarked stile and continue **straight ahead** along the side of the field. Climb over the stile and **turn right** along the fence. Continue downhill along the wooded track. **Turn right** at the field to continue down the hill. Follow the edge of the field round towards the church tower. Cross a stony farm track and walk through the gate opposite and towards the church. Pass a marker post and walk along a yew and beech hedge. **Head left** down the field and **right** through the churchyard.

11 Walk down the church steps past the old oak tree. Walk **straight ahead** along the lane. Stop for a Harvey's at The Salehurst Halt if you wish. Walk on along this sometimes residential lane using the verge and pavement where possible.

12 Continue **straight ahead** at the roundabout by using the pedestrian crossing on the right. Walk along Northbridge Street. This becomes The Clappers, thought to be the site of the original *Pons Roberti*. Cross the bridge and continue along the High Street. **Turn right** down Station Road towards the car parks.

BATTLE & ITS WIDER LANDSCAPE

DISTANCE: 13.8KM/8.6MILES » **TOTAL ASCENT**: 280M/917FT » **START GR**: TQ 747157 » **TIME**: ALLOW 4 HOURS PLUS STOPS
SATNAV: TN33 0AD » **MAP**: OS EXPLORER 124, HASTINGS & BEXHILL, 1:25,000 » **REFRESHMENTS**: VARIOUS IN BATTLE; THE
PLOUGH INN, CROWHURST » **NAVIGATION**: STRAIGHTFORWARD THANKS TO WELL-SIGNED SECTIONS OF THE 1066 COUNTRY
WALK AND BEXHILL LINK.

THE CLIMB UP BLACKHORSE HILL

18 **Battle & its Wider Landscape**   13.8km/8.6miles

This atmospheric route explores the undulating landscape around Battle Abbey and the renowned 1066 battlefields, taking in two very different woodlands and an ancient churchyard.

Battle Abbey » Great Wood » Blackhorse Hill » Crowhurst » Fore Wood RSPB Reserve » 1066 Country Walk Bexhill Link » Battle Abbey

Start

1066 Battle of Hastings, Abbey & Battlefield (paid) car park. GR: TQ 747157. Alternative start from Crowhurst Station (Point 10).

The Walk

Picnics are recommended for this walk, but another option is to walk early then enjoy lunch in Battle before exploring the abbey. The story goes that William the Conqueror founded Battle Abbey on the site of the Battle of Hastings as penance for the bloodshed, and our walk tries to give you a sense of the battlefield's location in the wider landscape. Contemporary sources, such as the Bayeux Tapestry and the chronicler William of Poitiers, inform our understanding of the Battle of Hastings. Harold's forces lined the ridge while the Normans were south on the other side of the marshy valley. Recent claims that the battle was fought at Crowhurst or Caldbec Hill are controversial but, as you walk, think of the thousands of soldiers who fought a momentous battle somewhere on these Sussex slopes.

The pavement stretch at the start enables us to leave the town through Great Wood, a vast coniferous woodland. Our path is straightforward but could be muddy in winter. Before long, we climb Blackhorse Hill on what is possibly an ancient sunken path, formed by early farmers droving their pigs. Years later, William's forces were thought to gather on Blackhorse and Telham hills, only a mile from Harold's army but hidden from sight. How would these gradients have felt to warriors approaching battle?

Later, nip into St George's churchyard to see the Crowhurst yew. The Ancient Yew group estimates that the tree was probably planted on this sacred site by the South Saxons. The tree features in a novel by Hope Muntz called *The Golden Warrior: 'Harold's fair manor at Crowhurst was burnt and the Reeve hanged from the great yew tree in the churchyard because he refused to tell where the treasure was hidden.'*

These days, RSPB reserve Fore Wood is so peaceful you might hear leaves whisper or an acorn drop. Ferns thrive in the shade of small steep-sided ravines in the sandstone: a typical High Weald gill.

18 BATTLE & ITS WIDER LANDSCAPE

Directions – Battle & its Wider Landscape

➲ Exit the car park on the footpath. Pass a 1066 Country Walk (1066 CW) signpost and walk towards Rye. **Turn right** past the abbey entrance. Follow the path that runs beneath the wall. Pass St Mary's church on the opposite roadside.

2 Cross the road at The Chequers. **Walk left** at the roundabout, continuing **straight ahead** along Marley Lane following the signed 1066 CW. Walk down the hill and cross the railway line at the crossing. Continue on. Cross a minor road and then, when the pavement ends, cross the road to walk on the other side. Cross Harrier Lane and walk along the verge. Pass Blackfriars Oast.

3 Beside the gate to Greatwood Cottage, **turn right** along the signed bridleway and follow the 1066 CW through Great Wood. Pass a signpost and continue **straight ahead** past two waymarked crossroads. At the bottom of a hill, cross a stony track and pass a bench.

4 After 50m, **turn right** along the signed 1066 CW which you will see just after a *Sedlescombe* marker post. Walk up this steepish track. **Keep right** at the next signpost, staying on the 1066 CW. Emerge on a golf course and **walk right** for a few metres. **Turn left** on to the track and bridleway at a 1066 CW marker stump and walk through the golf course. Look out for a waymarker stump: walk **straight ahead** on the bridleway towards the side of a hedge. Walk on through the opening along the fenced path.

5 **Turn right** at the signpost to walk along a bridleway, leaving the 1066 CW. Go through a waymarked opening in a fence corner and walk **straight ahead** down the side of the grassy fairway (!). Keep going until you reach the bottom where, without crossing the ditch, you continue **straight ahead**, crossing the woodchip track, to where the bridleway enters some woods.

6 Go through a gate and **walk right** up the large field along the unsigned bridleway. At the top, **go left** through the **second** metal gate (note bridleway arrow on other side of the post) and continue on the fenced track. After a bit of a climb, pass a post where you join a rough driveway. Continue **straight ahead** on this bridleway/driveway. Pass a modern oast house/circular building. Views to the right make you realise how high you've climbed; there's more to come …

7 At the road, **turn right** to walk along the grass verge. Cross to use the pavement. Pass a red-brick chapel.

8 **Turn left** along Telham Lane. **Turn left again** along the track to Brakes Coppice Farm and Crowhurst Park Cricket Club. Walk along this unsigned public footpath. This is easy walking with far-reaching views.

9 **Turn right** through the waymarked walkers' gate along the signed footpath in front of the private farmhouse. At the end of the fenced path, go through a gate, cross a drive (there's a handy bench here for a rest stop) and descend the signed footpath down some makeshift steps. At the bottom, follow the signed footpath **left** to join the tarmac track. The footpath soon crosses the drive to Brakes Coppice Park (camping) and then joins it higher up as you head over the plank bridge and **straight ahead** up the hill. Walk along this pleasant tree-lined drive and through a white gate.

10 **Turn left** along the lane. Pass Crowhurst Christian Healing Centre. **Turn left** along the footpath to Crowhurst Station. Cross over the railway bridge and walk **straight on** into the village. Walk down this quiet street which boasts an interesting mix of old and new homes.

11 At Forewood Lane, **turn right*** (or nip into St George's church to see the Crowhurst yew). Pass the school and the church as you follow the road round.

> *To divert approx. 500m to The Plough Inn at Crowhurst, **turn left** along Forewood Lane and then **turn left** along Chapel Hill. Retrace your steps to return.

12 **Turn left** round the gate at the waymarker signpost. This path leads to RSPB Fore Wood and then Battle on the 1066 CW Bexhill Link. Walk straight up the edge and then across the middle of the field on the footpath. Walk along a mud track which descends through woodland. Go through a gate, noting direction of arrow. Head **slightly diagonally right** across the field on the footpath. Cross the stile and enter Fore Wood nature reserve. Follow the main path through the woods. Keep **straight on** at the marker post where the footpaths fork. The path climbs past a possible timber storage area. Walk on along this main track, **ignoring** offshoots. Pass a 1066 CW marker stump and descend past another marker post to exit through a kissing gate.

Directions – Battle & its Wider Landscape continued…

13 Cross a footbridge and walk **straight ahead** along the fence. At the signpost, **walk right** and pass a gate.

14 **Turn right** along the signed bridleway and road at the path junction in front of Powdermill Cottage. Walk down the hill. Cross a bridge over a stream and cover some ground on this easy walking lane. Pass The Old Coach House and Peppering Eye Farm. Continue **straight ahead** on this lane.

15 **Walk left** at the road junction, continuing on the signed 1066 CW Bexhill Link. **Take care** on this short stretch of road. At the next junction, walk **straight ahead** from the traffic island to cross busy Powdermill Lane and pass a walkers' post signing mileage to Battle. Climb over a stile and walk along the fenced footpath which runs above the road. At the top, go through a gate. Cross a lane and carry on **straight ahead** through a metal gate following the 1066 CW Bexhill Link. See Battle ahead on the ridge? Pass a couple of marker posts. Soon, a fenced path climbs gradually towards the battlefield. Go through a couple of gates and continue to climb along the side of grazing fields. Pass a signpost and walk **straight ahead** on a mud track. There's a pretty stream to your left but was this field such an idyllic site when the battle raged? Although it is hard to be certain how nearby that might have been. Keep **straight ahead** at the marker post. Go through a walkers' gate by a wall. Walk on towards the abbey and **either turn right** for the car park **or go straight on** to visit the battlefield site within the abbey or a local cafe.

COUNTRYSIDE & COAST: HASTINGS

DISTANCE: 16.9KM/10.5MILES » **TOTAL ASCENT**: 528M/1,731FT » **START GR**: TQ 828094 » **TIME**: ALLOW 5–6 HOURS PLUS STOPS » **POSTCODE**: TN34 3DW » **MAP**: OS EXPLORER 124, HASTINGS & BEXHILL, 1:25,000 » **REFRESHMENTS**: THE TWO SAWYERS (BOOKING RECOMMENDED) AND THE TIC TOCORY TEA ROOM, PETT » **NAVIGATION**: TRICKY WITH A LOT OF HIGH STILES! ONE AMBIGUOUS STRETCH OF THE 1066 COUNTRY WALK AND SOME UNSIGNED FOOTPATHS SO USE MAP POINTS CAREFULLY WITH DIRECTIONS. NAVIGATION IN HASTINGS COUNTRY PARK IS HELPED BY NUMBERED MARKER POSTS: FOLLOW ADVISED DIVERSIONS.

A COASTAL PATH IN HASTINGS COUNTRY PARK

19 **Countryside & Coast: Hastings**   16.9km/10.5miles

To fully enjoy this challenging and varied trail, try an early start, a stop at a 16th-century pub, and plenty of time to meander back along the coast through the spectacular coves and gullies of Hastings Country Park.

Hastings Old Town » East Hill Lift » Barley Lane » Fairlight Hall » Pett » Fairlight » Fire Hills » Lower Warren Glen » Fairlight Glen » Ecclesbourne Glen » Barley Lane » Hastings Old Town

Start

Rock-a-Nore Road (paid) car park, Hastings Old Town. GR: TQ 828094. Alternative start, avoiding East Hill Lift, at Barley Lane car park (Point 4). GR: TQ 838104. TN35 5DX.

The Walk

'There were strange doings by night in the creeks and hollow ways and caves of the southern coast ... Every now and then a fisherman's boots were found to be stuffed with French lace, gloves, and jewellery, or a lady's petticoats to be quilted all through with silk stockings and lace.' The dark glens and hidden coves of this coastline were a boon for smugglers whose 19th-century exploits were chronicled by John Banks, a Hastings schoolteacher. This rewarding walk has much to recommend it: history, variety, atmospheric stony paths with mossy banks, and superb coastal walking along sandstone cliffs and through the glens of Hastings Country Park. However, the high stiles, sometimes tricky navigation, steep paths and unexpected diversions through the glens mean it may not be for everyone.

The full version starts in Hastings Old Town where you can wander past the restored 'net huts' and 'The Stade' (fish market) before a ride up the funicular railway. East Hill Lift dates from 1902 and, for a small fee, carries you up to Hastings Country Park.

Hastings Country Park covers five kilometres of spectacular soft cliffs and coastland and includes valuable habitats such as ancient gill woodland, heath and coastal grassland, and is home to rare vegetation, birds such as the black redstart and peregrine, dormice and invertebrates such as glowworms and the nationally scarce moth Webb's wainscot, plus many more species. A small number of Exmoor ponies and belted Galloway cattle graze the glens and slopes of this nature reserve for long-term sustainability. A small visitor centre is sometimes staffed by volunteers. The sandstone cliffs make this coast special, but they are also crumbling and unpredictable. Take warnings seriously. Pay attention to country park notices and expect changes to paths: suggested diversions take precedence over our directions.

19 COUNTRYSIDE & COAST: HASTINGS

Directions – Countryside & Coast: Hastings

➎ Walk **straight ahead** from the car park past the public toilets and through the old fishing town. Pass the Fishermen's Museum and a noticeboard for The Stade Trail. On your right, see the East Hill Lift. Ride the funicular! Or, to climb the steps instead, **turn right** after The Dolphin Inn up Tarnarisk Steps and **left** along Tackleway to climb up more steps which emerge beside the lift station.

2 **Turn right** up the steps following the Saxon Shore Way left along the cliff. Walk between clumps of undergrowth towards a marker post. **Walk left** to the left-hand marker for the Fish Trail and follow the leisure path.

3 Pass a Hastings Country Park (HCP) Nature Reserve post and see an HCP sign. Walk on past another Fish Trail marker and along a short cobbled stretch, past Rocklands Holiday Park and then straight along a tarmac bridleway. **Turn right** at the end of Rocklands Lane. Cross and walk along the pavement. Walk past Glenview Close.

4 Pass Barley Lane car park (alternative start). Stay on the road, passing Shear Barn reception. Climb the hill and pass some houses. Stay on this footpath and private street past the touring field. Walk **straight ahead** past gate 3 of HCP and a marker post showing *¾ mile to Fairlight Glen*. Pass a couple more marker posts, including marker post 11 for HCP and a National Cycle Network signpost.

SWEET PEAS ON A GARDEN FENCE NEAR THE ENTRANCE TO HASTINGS COUNTRY PARK

5 **Turn left** up a steep hill at a large HCP sign and noticeboard. Pass yellow gate 6.

6 Walk **diagonally left** across the road following the signed 1066 Country Walk (1066 CW). Cross the car park entrance. Go through the kissing gate towards North's Seat and head **diagonally left** across a grazing field.

7 Continue **straight on** through a kissing gate. Walk beside a fence and enjoy views towards the coast. **Turn right** through a 'split' fence and walk across a track to follow the 1066 CW. Walk down a grassy path with far-reaching views over patchwork fields towards the sea. Climb over a stile.

8 Cross the road and continue **straight ahead**, climbing over an obvious stile beside the drive to Fairlight Hall. **This section is tricky** because the official right of way, as marked on our map, can be unclear, but heads diagonally left though the crop field. To avoid spoiling crops, a common sense approach is to walk down the edge of the field, in which case, at the stile into the woods, **turn left** to follow the 1066 CW, as shown on the marker post, across the field on a rough mud track. When you are almost at the gap in the hedge, **turn right** to join another mud track and continue down the field. Enjoy clear views of Fairlight Hall to your right. When you hit another perpendicular mud track, **turn left** and walk through a gap in a line of trees and then immediately **turn right** past an electricity post and then **turn and walk diagonally left** across the field towards a dark gap in the trees.

9 At the marker post, walk into the trees along a waymarked footpath, an old stony path with mossy banks. Cross a couple of footbridges. Go up some steps and across a glade, perhaps rich in seasonal wild flowers. Cross a track with a 1066 CW marker post and walk **straight ahead** through a kissing gate and along the footpath through a crop field. Go through a gate and follow the 1066 CW **straight ahead** along a fence. Look right and see St Andrew's church tower. Go through another gate and continue to walk along a fence. Glimpse the sea ahead and see a lake at the bottom of the hill to your right. Cross over a stile and walk through a copse. Climb a stile into a grazing field and walk **straight on**. Climb over a double stile. Walk **straight ahead** across the field on the footpath. Climb over a stile.

10 Cross a road and the track to Winterstow Cottages and climb over a stile. Walk **straight ahead** on the waymarked footpath. Cross over another stile and walk on. You can't help but notice an unusually tiled house to the right. Climb over another stile. Cross the lane. Climb over a stile and walk along the fenced footpath alongside grazing fields. Climb over a stile and follow a mud track through Roughter's Wood. The path heads roughly straight on and passes several marker posts. It begins to climb and eventually becomes quite steep as it curves left along a fence.

11 Emerge in Pett, opposite The Two Sawyers. **Turn right** to walk along the road, passing the Tic Tocory tea room. Pass St Mary and St Peter's church.

12 **Turn right** just beyond the churchyard wall, following the signed footpath. Cross a stile and walk **straight ahead** and then, at the corner, **diagonally left** through a grazing field to a marker post. Cross a stile and walk down a hill along a fenced path with lovely views of a hill. Cross another stile and continue down the edge of the field. Follow the line of the post and wire fence. Cross a waymarked stile, pass a boulder and continue on **straight ahead**. Climb over another stile and walk **straight ahead** down a slope and through a grazing field. At the marker post, **walk straight ahead**. Soon, cross a footbridge with stiles and walk up the footpath along the edge of a grazing field. Pass a stile in the hedge and continue on and up to the top.

13 Cross an elaborate stile and walk **diagonally left**. Cross a rudimentary stile by the metal gate into a fenced area. **Walk right** towards the lane. **Turn right** along the tarmac track and public footpath.

14 Take a few steps to the **right** and then **turn left** to climb over a stile. Walk **straight ahead** along the fence and round the field to the waymarked signpost by the gate. Follow the public footpath through the gate and turn **diagonally left** along the signed footpath. Continue **straight on** through the next field, a grassland. **Ignore** gates into the woods. Walk on and then near the end of the field, walk **diagonally right** to the corner beside a thatched cottage. Climb over a waymarked stile, walk a few steps and go round a waymarked gate. Follow the footpath **right** along the drive.

15 Cross the road and walk **straight ahead** on the public footpath with the *No Entry* sign for bikes. **Turn left** at the residential road.

16 **Walk right** along the pavement on this road through Fairlight. Climb the hill. Pass The Cove and a bus stop. Go **straight ahead** at the roundabout. Go up the hill.

17 Reach the sea, Channel Way and the Saxon Shore Way. **Turn right** and walk along the coastal path past some houses.

18 Enter Hastings Country Park (HCP) through a gate and walk to a noticeboard. The sandstone cliffs make this nature reserve a unique landscape, but do heed warnings as they are crumbling and unpredictable. We follow a diversion in Fairlight Cove and **recommend you pay attention** to country park notices and take diversions if necessary. Pass *HCP marker post 27* and walk on to climb up along a steep grassy track. **Turn left** along a gravel track by a picnic bench and enjoy wonderful views of the English Channel.

19 At *marker post 25*, **turn diagonally left** through the scrub and on up to pass a noticeboard by artist Julian Hanshaw. Continue to the **left** of a mobile phone mast and walk down **diagonally left** to a gate.

20 At *marker post 24*, go through a kissing gate to Warren Glen Lower. This path with rough steps has great views of an intricate coastline and some handy benches, great for a well-earned refreshment stop. In season, these cliffs may be grazed by ponies and cattle. Descend for a while. At *marker post 22*, **turn left** down some steps and follow the track. Cross a bridge over a stream. Pass a marker post and *Dangerous Cliffs* sign and climb a very steep hill. At the top, you may stop at a handy bench. Walk along the fence.

Directions – Countryside & Coast: Hastings continued…

21 Go through a gate and pass *marker post 18*. Climb a steep track with a lot of steps. Emerge in a clifftop clearing and walk on along the fence. Descend. More steps! At *marker post 17*, **turn left** to descend further towards the sea and Fairlight Glen. Walk on down more steps through a very atmospheric wood. Pass beach access – **not currently advised** due to rockfalls (!). Cross a bridge over the stream and climb to regain your height. At the unlabelled marker post, **walk left** upwards. Climb some steps and pass *marker post 14*. Climb lots more steps! Are these ancient cobbled paths, used by fishermen and their families or perhaps smugglers and excise men?

22 At *marker post 12*, **go left** towards Ecclesbourne Glen. Although you may notice another route to Barley Lane is signed right, our path offers sea views and the path leads you through gorse and ferns. Walk **straight on** at *marker post 8*. Walk along a fenced path until you reach a viewpoint. **Turn right** along the footpath. Go down some steps with a good view of the sandstone cliffs. *Sections of Ecclesbourne Glen are closed at time of writing due to rockfalls and landslides so we follow an HCP diversion. Look out for HCP trail advice as the landscape is not stable.* **Turn right** at the marker post with a diversion arrow and down some more steps. Walk along this very uneven rocky path (!). Pass some boulders and cross a footbridge. **Turn right** and up the track. Cross another waymarked footbridge across what feels like a rocky enchanted glen and continue up some rocky steps (!). **Walk left** down the slope when you emerge on to an unsigned track. At *marker post 7*, walk **straight ahead** towards Barley Lane car park. More steps and a climb.

23 Go through a kissing gate into Barley Lane car park. **Turn left** along the bridleway and road. **Walk left** along Rocklands Lane. Retrace your steps to the funicular. If the lift is closed, go down the adjacent steps to Tackleway. **Turn left** and **then right** down Tamarisk Steps. Rock-a-Nore is signed.

WATERWAYS & WIDE-OPEN SPACES OF THE ROTHER VALLEY

DISTANCE: 22.4KM/13.9MILES » **TOTAL ASCENT:** 137M/448FT » **START GR:** TQ 897269 » **TIME:** ALLOW 5.5–6 HOURS PLUS STOPS
POSTCODE: TN30 7EA » **MAP:** OS EXPLORER 125, ROMNEY MARSH, RYE & WINCHELSEA, 1:25,000 » **REFRESHMENTS:** THEATRE
CAFE AT NATIONAL TRUST SMALLHYTHE PLACE; THE FERRY INN (RECOMMENDED, BOOKING ESSENTIAL AT WEEKENDS), STONE IN OXNEY;
OXNEY GOURMET PIE AND BURGER BAR, WITTERSHAM » **NAVIGATION:** MAINLY WELL-ESTABLISHED TRAILS EXCEPT AMBIGUOUS
SECTIONS IN POINTS 9 AND 13. PLEASE FOLLOW ANY SIGNED PATH DIVERSIONS AS RIGHTS OF WAY MAY ALTER.

20 Waterways & Wide-Open Spaces of the Rother Valley

22.4km/13.9miles

An extensive but flattish loop with easy navigation including long sections along the River Rother, the Royal Military Canal and the High Weald Landscape Trail.

Wittersham » Smallhythe Place » Reading Sewer » Luckhurst » The Ferry Inn » Stone in Oxney » St Mary's Church » Stone Cliff » Royal Military Canal » River Rother » Wittersham

Start

Roadside parking in front of St John the Baptist church, Wittersham.
GR: TQ 897269.

The Walk

This walk begins with a meandering stretch of the High Weald Landscape Trail through sheep fields. The Reading Sewer dyke is the old Rother, once an important transport link between Rye and Tenterden turning Small Hythe into a thriving port and ship-building centre. National Trust property Smallhythe Place stands proudly by the riverside, its displays inspired by the theatrical lives of Victorian actress Ellen Terry and later her daughter, Edith (or 'Edy') Craig, a suffragette.

The old Rother became silted and reverted to its original course via the Isle of Oxney – now Stone in Oxney. By the end of the 18th century only barges and small boats could reach Small Hythe. Throughout this area history underlines how the changing courses of waterways alter the fortunes of settlements. The village of Stone in Oxney, then the Isle of Oxney, was ransacked by the Danes in 994. Today, 15th-century St Mary's

church is well worth a visit, and not just for its atmospheric location and appealing views over the valley.

Stone Cliff lies on the edge of the Rother Levels and is a fascinating section of abandoned cliff line, or old coast, and a wonderful viewpoint towards a now-distant sea. There is much to enjoy on this walk but the long stretches of easy-to-navigate paths ensure you can walk at a good pace and take the time to stop and explore what interests you.

We include a short section of the 28-mile Royal Military Canal Path. Its creation was a gruelling task for the navvies who worked by hand with picks and shovels, but they were probably grateful to have work. Our walk concludes with a long stretch along the banks of the River Rother, home to fishermen, occasional dayboats and water-loving creatures. Fish splash, a cuckoo calls and birds of prey swoop in the skies above but, in our time, the river is quiet.

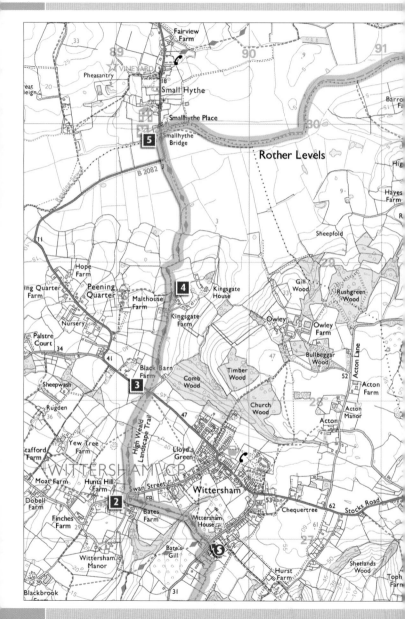

Rother Levels

WITTERSHAM CP

Wittersham

CONTINUES ON PAGE 163

20 WATERWAYS & WIDE-OPEN SPACES OF THE ROTHER VALLEY (1)

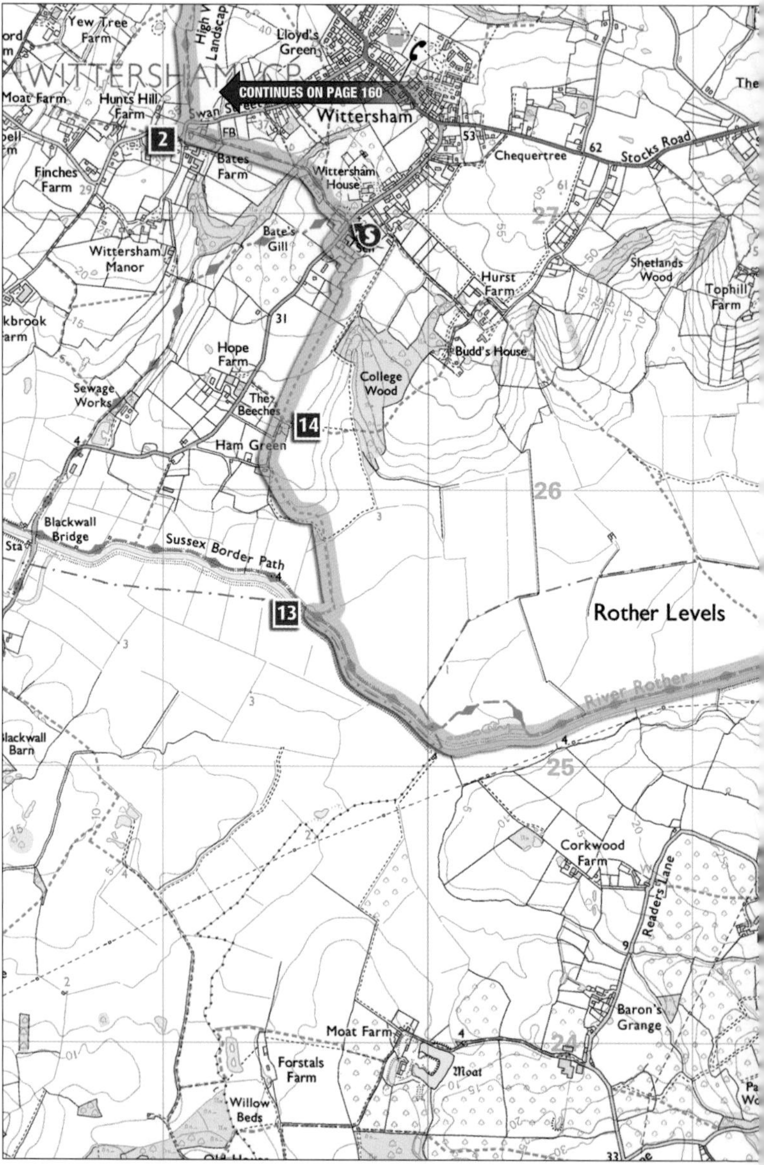

CONTINUES ON PAGE 160

20 WATERWAYS & WIDE-OPEN SPACES OF THE ROTHER VALLEY (2)

Directions – Waterways & Wide-Open Spaces of the Rother Valley

➲ Walk along the signed footpath opposite the church tower. Pass an apple orchard. Keep going on this path and walk past the atmospheric old churchyard. Go down some steps, across a waymarked footbridge over an idyllic stream and up some steps. Climb over a stile. Walk **straight ahead** along a fence. Climb over a stile and continue along a fenced path, passing a waymarker arrow on a fence post.

2 At the lane, **turn right** along the signed High Weald Landscape Trail (HWLT). Go round the corner and turn **left** at the HWLT signpost along the fenced footpath. At the end, go through a waymarked kissing gate and walk **straight ahead**. Go through another waymarked kissing gate and walk **straight ahead** along the waymarked public footpath. Near the ruined building, walk **straight on** past a waymarked post. Climb over the stile.

3 At the signpost, cross the road. Follow the tarmac lane as it curves past a house and onwards. Enjoy far-reaching views over patchwork fields. Walk **straight ahead** on the public footpath through Kingsgate Farm passing through a waymarked walkers' gate. After the black timber-boarded house, **turn left** to walk along the fenced footpath. Mind the roots. Go through the kissing gate.

4 **Turn left** to walk along the waymarked footpath. See the houses of Small Hythe in the distance. Go through a wide metal gate in the bottom corner of the field. See a waymarked marker post and **turn right** to walk along the hedge through the sheep field. **Turn left** at the marker post before you go through the gate, and walk along the perpendicular hedge. At the marker post, **turn right** and walk through the gate and along the fenced footpath. **Turn left** to walk through a wide gate and onwards through a grazing field. Go **straight on** through a waymarked gate. Walk on towards the road. Use the waymarked walkers' step to help you climb over the gate. **Turn right** to walk along the road and signed HWLT. Cross Smallythe Bridge and visit NT Smallhythe Place if you wish.

5 **Turn right** along the signed bridleway on the same side of the river as Smallhythe Place for 3.2km. About halfway, cross a footbridge and continue on along the river. Stay on this side at the locked gate, following the river as it curves left. See Ramsden Nurseries to your distant left. Cross a wooden footbridge and continue on. Go through a gate.

6 **Turn right** along the lane for a few steps and **then left** along the signed bridleway to keep walking in roughly the same direction. Walk along the tarmac track to Chapel Bank Farm. The bridleway curves right by the barn and then left. Follow the track until you see a marker post. **Turn left** along the grassy bridleway. At the next marker post, **turn right** along the bridleway beside the river.

7 Stop before Ebony Pumping Station. **Turn right*** along the grassy footpath beside a smaller water channel/drainage ditch. This is Saxon Shore Way (SSW). At the marker post **turn left** across a footbridge. At the farm, walk **straight on** but pass to the **right** of the unwaymarked fence before you go past the liquid tanks and large corrugated iron barns. Cross a stile, opposite the barns, with an SSW arrow and walk **straight ahead** through the grazing field. Climb over the stile at the SSW signpost.

> **OR** *If you wish to stop at the Ferry Inn, follow the bridleway **straight on**: you can see this rather nice inn in the distance.

8 You are at Luckhurst. Walk **straight ahead** over the lane on the SSW. Go through the brick gateposts, past a lovely house with muted red bricks, and **straight on** past the stone footpath marker. **Turn left** at the marker post (currently fallen over) across the footbridge and walk **diagonally left** along the SSW. (If the path isn't obvious through this crop field you may prefer to walk right and then left round the field edge.)

9 From the marker post and path junction, walk **slightly left**, keeping the ditch and line of coppiced trees on your right. Walk on along the hedgerow and into a new field where you walk **diagonally right** towards a gate and the village. Cross a stile.

10 You are in Stone in Oxney opposite The Crown Inn (currently closed). Cross the road and follow the unsigned SSW along the road towards the stone church. Pass the memorial hall. Stay on this quiet lane passing several signposts for footpaths. Use the verge where appropriate. Walk up Church Hill and make sure you visit the churchyard. Continue to the top of the road. Climb the hill and enjoy views towards the coast.

Directions – Waterways & Wide-Open Spaces of the Rother Valley continued...

11 At the road junction, walk **straight ahead** through a kissing gate to follow the signed SSW. Walk along the fence and through a signed kissing gate. Walk **diagonally left** towards the sea, which you can glimpse in the distant vista. Go through a waymarked kissing gate and continue **diagonally left** down the hill towards the waterway. Go through a kissing gate and down past Stone Cliff, a fascinating geological site formed from ancient cliffs and coastline. Go through the waymarked kissing gate beside the gate and take the centre path towards the wind farm and sea. Watch your step as the ground is uneven underfoot. Go through a kissing gate and across a footbridge. Walk **slightly left** but **stay to the right of the watery ditch**. Walk on and cross the grass and stone bridge to continue on along the side of the ditch. Join the stony track and continue **straight ahead**. At the brick shed, leave the track to continue **straight ahead** on the mud track to the left of a ditch. At the end, **turn right** across a grassy bridge and along a waterway. Go through a narrow gap and cross the flat bridge to the road.

12 Cross the road to follow the signed SSW. Climb over a stile and **turn right** to walk along the footpath beside the Royal Military Canal. Path uneven: watch your step. Climb over a stile and **turn left** to walk on along the road for a few steps. Cross the road. **Easy to miss: turn right** at an old waymarked gatepost to walk round a metal gate and along the footpath. **Turn right** at the corner to follow this stony and grassy bridleway along the River Rother for almost 5km. Walk past Craven Pumping Station. Walk through two gates, each beside a birdhouse. Walk on and through a third gate. Pass some boat moorings and go through another gate. Walk on until the road bridge where you exit through a walkers' gate. Cross Wittersham Road by Eccles Turf. Go through two walkers' gates by Newbridge North Pumping Station. Continue **straight ahead** along this scenic stretch of the River Rother. Go through a gate and walk on along the Sussex Border Path. Pass a pumping station on the other side and go ahead though a waymarked kissing gate. Walk on.

13 At the marker post, **turn right** up and over the bank along the footpath. Walk along beside the stream. **Go left** at the next marker post to cross a grassy bridge across the watery ditch. Walk along the footpath, keeping **left** of the next, different, ditch. Ahead, you will be pleased to spot the distant square tower of St John the Baptist church. **Keep left** at the fork on entering the next field. The footpath is not signed or clear through the field but, after the first bend, it runs initially roughly 10m parallel above the track, and then cuts diagonally left to rejoin the track by the first house.

14 Without going through the locked gate across the track, **walk right** on the waymarked grassy footpath along the hedge/boundary. At the end of the hedge, **turn right** away from a house and stile. Walk towards the church tower on the grassy footpath along the line of telephone wires. Pass a waymarker post and walk on along the hedge through the next field. At the end, **turn left** at the waymarker post to walk along the fenced footpath. Climb over a stile. **Turn right** and walk along the road past the oast house and school.

VIEW ACROSS STONE CLIFF TOWARDS THE ROTHER LEVELS

DAY WALKS GUIDEBOOKS

Written by local authors, each pocket-sized guidebook features:

- 20 great day-length walks
- Ordnance Survey 1:25,000-scale maps
- easy-to-follow directions
- distance & navigation information
- refreshment stops & local area information
- a detailed appendix

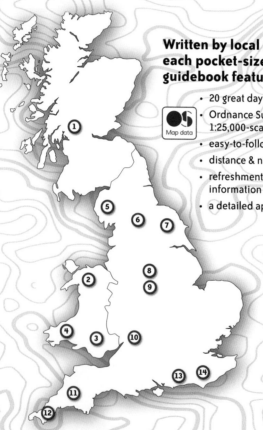

Available from book shops or direct from:
www.v-publishing.co.uk

Appendix

The following is a list of Tourist Information Centres, shops, cafes, pubs, websites and other contacts that might come in handy.

Tourist Information Centres

www.highweald.org – official website for the High Weald.

East Grinstead	T: 01342 410 121
Hastings	T: 01424 451 111
Horsham	T: 01403 211 661
Rye	T: 01797 226 696
Tonbridge	T: 01732 770 929
Tunbridge Wells	T: 01892 515 675

Food and Drink
CAFES

The list below is not exhaustive; see individual routes for recommendations.

Weeks Bakery and Tea Rooms, Goudhurst	T: 01580 211 380
Community Shop and Cafe, Benenden	T: 01580 279 808
Tablehurst Farm Cafe, Forest Row	T: 01342 823 173
Bolney Wine Estate Cafe and Shop	T: 01444 881 575
Barn Cafe, National Trust Standen House	T: 01342 323 029
Taffels, Forest Row	T: 01342 458 070
Piglet's Tearoom, Pooh Corner, Hartfield	T: 01892 770 456
Theatre Cafe, National Trust Smallhythe Place	T: 01580 762 334
The Tic Tocory, Pett	T: 01424 814 554
Wharf Tea Room, National Trust Bodiam	T: 01580 830 196
The Pink Cabbage Produce Company, Mayfield	T: 01435 872 557
Borde Hill Gardens Cafes	T: 01444 450 326
Waterfront Cafe, Bewl Water Visitor Centre	T: 01892 893 931

Coach House Tea Room, Hole Park Gardens	T: 01580 241 344
Barnsgate Manor Restaurant and Tea Room	T: 01825 713 366
Mulberry Tea Room, National Trust Bateman's	T: 01435 882 302
Fellows Bakery, Ardingly	T: 01444 892 257

PUBS

The list below is not exhaustive; see individual routes for recommendations.

The Old Dunnings Mill, East Grinstead	T: 01342 821 080
Oxney Gourmet Pie and Burger Bar, Wittersham	T: 01797 270 913
The Bull at Benenden	T: 01580 240 054
The Salehurst Halt, Salehurst	T: 01580 880 620
The Cat Inn, West Hoathly	T: 01342 810 369
Castle Inn, Bodiam	T: 01580 830 330
The George Inn, Robertsbridge	T: 01580 880 315
The Plough Inn, Crowhurst	T: 01424 830 310
The Half Moon, Warninglid	T: 01444 461 227
The Dragon, Colgate	T: 01293 851 286
The Pig & Butcher, Five Ash Down	T: 01825 732 191
The Ferry Inn, Stone in Oxney	T: 01233 758 246
The Two Sawyers, Pett	T: 01424 812 255
The Middle House, Mayfield	T: 01435 872 146
The Rose & Crown, Mayfield	T: 01435 872 200
The Woodcock Inn, Iden Green	T: 01580 240 009
The Victory Inn, Staplefield	T: 01444 400 463
The Jolly Tanners, Staplefield	T: 01444 400 335
The Horse & Cart Inn, Peasmarsh	T: 01797 230 034
The Bull Inn, Ticehurst	T: 01580 200 586
The Old Vine Inn, Cousley Wood	T: 01892 782 271
The Half Moon Inn, Balcombe	T: 01444 811 582
Dorset Arms, Withyham	T: 01892 770 278
The Foresters Arms, Fairwarp	T: 01825 712 808
The Bull Inn, Rolvenden	T: 01580 241 212
The Junction Inn, Groombridge	T: 01892 864 275
The Wheel Inn, Burwash Weald	T: 01435 882 299
The Vine, Goudhurst	T: 01580 211 105

The Star and Eagle, Goudhurst .... T: 01580 211 512
The Ardingly Inn, Ardingly .... T: 01444 892 214
The Anchor Inn, Hartfield .... T: 01892 770 424
The Nevill Crest and Gun,
Eridge Green .... T: 01892 864 209
The Hurstwood, High Hurstwood ..... T: 01825 732 257
The Bear Inn, Burwash .... T: 01435 882 540
The Rose and Crown, Burwash .... T: 01435 882 600
The Gun & Spitroast, Horsmonden .. T: 01892 722 925
The Ewe & Lamb, Rolvenden Layne .. T: 01580 241 837

Accommodation
YOUTH HOSTELS
While there are no YHA youth hostels within the
High Weald area, the following can be found relatively
close by in Sussex. For more information please visit:
www.yha.org.uk

Eastbourne .... T: 0345 371 9316
South Downs .... T: 0345 371 9574

HOTELS, B&BS AND SELF-CATERING
www.visitsoutheastengland.com/accommodation
For further information, contact a Tourist Information
Centre in the area in which you intend to stay.

Camping
www.campsites.co.uk .... www.coolcamping.com
For more information, contact a local Tourist
Information Centre.

Weather
www.metoffice.gov.uk
Provides a seven-day weather forecast for places
in the High Weald.

Outdoor Shops
Just a selection. There are many more
in the South East area.

Cotswold Outdoor, Horsham .... T: 01403 858 312
www.cotswoldoutdoor.com

Camping World, Horsham .... T: 01403 255 458
www.campingworld.co.uk

Go Outdoors, Tonbridge .... T: 0344 387 6762
www.gooutdoors.co.uk

Millets, Tunbridge Wells .... T: 01892 574 891
www.millets.co.uk

Other Publications
Day Walks on the South Downs
Deirdre Huston, Vertebrate Publishing.
www.v-publishing.co.uk

Sussex Walks
Deirdre Huston, Vertebrate Publishing.
www.v-publishing.co.uk

Cycling Days Out: South East England
Deirdre Huston, Vertebrate Publishing.
www.v-publishing.co.uk

Cycling in Sussex
Deirdre Huston & Marina Bullivant, Vertebrate Publishing.
www.v-publishing.co.uk

South East Mountain Biking: North & South Downs
Nick Cotton, Vertebrate Publishing.
www.v-publishing.co.uk

About the Author

Deirdre Huston is an author and photographer whose work is inspired by a love of history, literature and the outdoors. She is a graduate of the MA in creative writing at Bath Spa University and also writes fiction. As well as shooting stills photography, she has made films exploring the history of Saddlescombe, a National Trust downland farm. She co-authored *Cycling in Sussex*, her first guidebook for Vertebrate Publishing, back in 2008 and has gone on to write and photograph *Sussex Walks*, *Day Walks on the South Downs* and *Cycling Days Out: South East England*.

Deirdre was born in Crawley on the fringes of the High Weald and now lives beside the South Downs in Sussex with her husband, three children and dog. For further details of her current projects, walking festivals or photography/creative writing workshops, please visit: **www.deirdrehuston.co.uk**

Vertebrate Publishing

At Vertebrate Publishing we publish books to inspire adventure.

It's our rule that the only books we publish are those that we'd want to read or use ourselves. We endeavour to bring you beautiful books that stand the test of time and that you'll be proud to have on your bookshelf for years to come.

The Peak District was the inspiration behind our first books. Our offices are situated on its doorstep, minutes away from world-class climbing, biking and hillwalking. We're driven by our own passion for the outdoors, for exploration, and for the natural world; it's this passion that we want to share with our readers.

We aim to inspire everyone to get out there. We want to connect readers – young and old – with the outdoors and the positive impact it can have on well-being. We think it's particularly important that young people get outside and explore the natural world, something we support through our publishing programme.

As well as publishing award-winning new books, we're working to make available many out-of-print classics in both print and digital formats. These are stories that we believe are unique and significant; we want to make sure that they continue to be shared and enjoyed.
www.v-publishing.co.uk